PDXccentric

An Odyssey of
PORTLAND Oddities

AIMEE WADE & SCOTT COOK

All photography (unless otherwise credited) and text:
Scott Cook and Aimee Wade.

Design, layout and printing by Jody Conners and Gary Asher of Maverick Publications, Bend Oregon.

Maps supplied by Jon Kelter Gehrig of Cascadia Geospatial.

Email Aimee for all sales inquiries: pdxccentric@gmail.com

Cover Photo: NW Cornell Road bike lane stencil (C4).

<u>Disclaimer.</u> The authors cannot be held responsible for any injury suffered due to the use of this guidebook. Don't blame us if you gag on our puns or if you tweak your curiosity or get your funny bone tickled. We can take no responsibility for any pain in the ass you suffer through the reading or using of this guidebook.

USING THIS GUIDE

First off, we've divided the city into five "quadrants", but not the five quadrants the city is usually divided into. Our quadrants are divided in such a way to help us map our entries so that our section maps are the most helpful they can be. We've used the back cover of the book as sort of a visual table of contents, showing you where the quadrants are and the extent of the entries and appendix listings in each section of the city.

Looking at the edge of the book you'll see we've tabbed the pages according to the sections of the book. Section A, is (duh), the first tab. See how easy we've made everything? Each section of the city has its own map which shows the numbered entries that are on the pages that follow, as well as the icons for the things that appear in our appendices.

For each entry in the book there is a topper box which has a street address and Google Coordinates. You can type either of these addresses into a smartphone, or you can get one of the old-school paper map thingies to try to find your way around.

The Appendices at the end of the book are a few PDX eccentricities that have multiple locations and thus would benefit by having a map of said locations. Each section map shows icons for the appendix features that are located in that section, but you'll have to look to the appendix lists for the exact addresses for all the various locations throughout the city.

Nearby (in the topper-box of each entry), is used to point out things from our appendices that are nearby when you are at that particular entry. It might also call out entry in a different section of the book. The Nearby numbers will refer to which appendix and the listing's number within the appendix.

Curiouser? If our entry tweaks your curiosity to learn more, we try to give you a nudge in the right directions here. This nudge might be a book to read, an online source for more detailed information, YouTube videos, or Portland movies from our list to watch. Our website will be a good place to get Curiouser too as we have links to most of the online information mentioned, endless newspaper and magazine clippings, additional color photos and much more.

The Bird. Well, we decided to put a bird on it too. Maybe put a bird on every page. Too much! We got sick of the bird and flipped the bird at the bird. We liked flipping the bird at the bird. We decided you might like to flip the bird too.

 So...we put the bird back on every page. Go ahead Portland, flip the bird!

USING THIS GUIDE

Extras:

Website. We have a website set up to parallel and enhance the guidebook entries. This website, hosted at www.PDXccentric.wordpress.com, has a page for each book entry, ordered correspondingly. The purpose of the website is to give "the rest of the story" so to speak. This includes all the extra photos, historic photos, newspaper articles, links to other online sources, videos, etc etc, that we feel will enhance the entry. The website will always be a "work in progress," knowing that there will always be extra info that comes to light about our entries, especially once we go to print and people fire comments and perspective back our way.

Facebook. We have a Facebook identity as PDXccentric Guidebook. Friend us to follow along our weekly stream of eccentricities, or to get in touch and share stuff.

Google Earth Panoramio. We've uploaded heaps of photos to GE's Panoramio so if you go digital searching, say for intersection murals, you'll find our on-the-ground photos to help enhance your citywide armchair travelings.

Amazon.com. We will sell *PDXccentric* on Amazon.com, but we know most all of our books will be sold through local PDX shops. But, Amazon matters to us for hosting reviews of our book. Please review our book on Amazon, even if you most likely didn't purchase it on Amazon. A review is the best way to help us succeed with our book, knowing that most people will check the online reviews before they purchase the book wherever they first see it.

Email us. Let us know what you think, what we got wrong, what we got right. Maybe you worked on the movie sets we have questions about. Maybe you took pix of *Portlandia* coming down the river. Maybe you danced at Zorba the Buddha disco. Maybe maybe maybe…we want your stories, your photos…your perspective…your Portland. If you have PDX-centric stuffs that directly pertain to our eccentric entries, we'll be happy to hear about it and share the stuff if you'd let us. PDXccentric@gmail.com

Scott:

I've never lived in Portland.

Out of college I worked a corporate job for British Petroleum for seven years. I didn't like it too much and finally quit outright, with no other job on my horizon. In 1998, after being "retired" for four years, I moved out of my van and into Hood River for the windsurfing possibilities. Appreciatively. I found the entire Columbia Gorge a far more fascinating place than I had imagined. In just a few years in Hood River I had decided to "un-retire" and write my own outdoors guidebook to the Gorge because the kind of guidebook that I wanted to buy just hadn't been written yet.

In 2002 I released my first self-published guidebook—*Curious Gorge*. The "curious" in the title said it all—my curiosity led me to find the many quirky oddities that I sprinkled into my guidebook, the stuff typical hiking guides don't feature. *Curious Gorge* proved a big hit, so I immediately started on a guidebook to the Bend area, an area that I thought I knew well. Turns out I didn't know Bend very well at all, but I sure was curious so I dug in and got digging and exploring and learning…and compiled it all into *Bend, Overall* in 2004.

In 2006 I visited New Zealand on a vacation, didn't like the outdoors books I found there, so decided to write my own. By 2010, after four three-month visits to NZ, I released two *NZ Frenzy* guidebooks, now both selling well with great reviews on Amazon. It seems that if I can't find the kind of guidebook I'd want to buy, I just set out to write it myself. If a place "wows" me, then digging-in to discover its secrets is a challenging adventure and a ton of fun and people seem to like my style and I seem to make a good living doing it. Kinda nice.

OK, so back to Portland. I began visiting PDX more and more often to sell my guidebooks. All throughout PDX I'd drive, delivering to Powell's, New Seasons, Whole Foods, sport stores, etc etc. The more I got to know Portland, the more intrigued I became, even though I had never been a "city guy." Picking up the *Willamette Week*, *Portland Mercury*, *Portland Monthly* and the like always gave me little extra snippets of PDX to check-out during my rounds. My curiosity grew. Vanport? Witch's Castle? Bart Simpson etching? Bubblers? Portlandia? Then I found Chuck Palahniuk's *Fugitives & Refugees*. Wow, this was a guidebook meant for me—a whole treasure-trove of curiosities! My book-delivery trips to PDX became more and more interesting—Stark's Vacuum Museum, Church of Elvis, Velveteria, Voodoo. Even so, I was just a curious tourist.

For me, Portland changed radically when I met Aimee Wade and we began dating in 2010. I'd arrive at her house in North Portland with a laundry-list of curiosities in my head, waiting to be explored. Surprisingly, I found that Aimee loved to go on little urban exploration adventures just as much as myself. Her curiosity, once whetted, proved as inquisitive as mine and off we'd go chasing-down the oddities mentioned in *Fugitives* or other sources. Our very first urban adventure-date was to find the Bart Simpson sidewalk etching that I had been told about. I didn't even know where Lincoln High School was, but she did, so off we went…and we found it! (The first-time-there pic is in entry C8). Portland became far more exciting to me with a sexy accomplice like Aimee to scout-out the odd and hidden. Together we discovered blogs like *Cyclotram* and *Café Unknown* which both gave us ever more to be curious about. How come nobody had written a guidebook with all these hidden goodies in it, other than *Fugitives & Refugees*—that's the book I wanted to buy!

Together we learned so many fascinating stories that hid behind so many PDX oddities. The White Stag sign…Lovejoy Columns…Mill Ends…Ghost Ramps…Harbor Drive…Willamette Stone. Having a partner as curious about everything as myself, I suggested to Aimee, in early 2013, that maybe she could go part-time and then we could write a guidebook together. I'd be the "ideas guy" and she'd be the "archives digger." I'd write the words, she'd compile the website…I'd coordinate the printing, she'd do all the photography. She decided not to go part-time…instead she just quit...to become a guidebook author! Aimee amazed me week after week, digging hidden nuggets out of obscure resources, "going beyond Google" as we liked to say. These were the very sorts of stories and tidbits that I knew would make our guidebook unique. Aimee deserves **all** the credit for digging-up the tales behind Mill Ends, Witch's Castle, Bart Simpson, Vanport Vestiges, etc, etc. I never once set foot in the Portland City Archives, Historical Society, *Willamette Week* office, or library microfiche room. I'd come up with ideas like "What did Dick Fagan *actually write* about Mill Ends park"…and then Aimee would dig-dig-dig until she'd often find a very surprising answer. From *Louie Louie* to the Willamette Stone, from Kelly Butte to Sauvie Island… 'round and 'round we explored and learned. Then we found Bike Lane guys, then we found intersection murals…and then we began to watch Portland-made movies…and then...and then…

AUTHORS' NOTES

And then we crunched it all together into this guidebook. It wasn't easy, no way, not at all. This was, BY FAR, the most difficult guidebook I'd ever attempted to write. I had no idea how easy it was to write about trails and waterfalls, lakes and rivers compared to trying to write about Portland's history, events, artistic endeavors, and peoples' accomplishments. Portland stories had "facts" and history and people involved…which is a lot harder to "get right" and tell the whole story, than telling hikers how to walk a trail to a waterfall. Honestly, finalizing this book has been a bitch—far more difficult, but also far more satisfying than my previous outdoors guidebooks. Portland has definitely changed for me forever. I love Portland, but even more than that, I have a respect for Portland's history and the people who have been involved in Portland's "renaissance" since the 1960s. To sum it all up maybe…I say "whoop whoop" all the time nowadays. It's been a fun trip to learn all this. Hope you like our version of it.

Aimee:

I was born and raised in Oregon and moved to Portland in 2000. For almost ten years I worked in nutrition/supplements at Whole Foods Market. In 2008 I met Scott at Whole Foods when we began carrying *Curious Gorge*. In 2010, after a book signing I orchestrated, Scott and I went out to talk shop and we hit it off. Shortly afterward we started dating. One of the first things I noticed about Scott was that he wondered about everything he saw and encountered. "How did that rock get there?" "Why is this place called Mock's Crest?" "If *Portlandia* was chosen by contest, what didn't win?" He was just like his book, "curious." Strangely, I was *not* very curious myself, seemingly never questioning anything. However, his curiosity immediately rubbed off on me. He would ask endless questions about Portland and I became obsessed with getting answers. If Scott had moved to the Gorge in 1995 and by 2002 he was writing a guidebook about it, what excuse did I have for not having the answers for Portland? For me it really helped having an iPhone handy. I began to find out that history is so much more accessible and fun to get at than ever before because of the Internet.

For years, Scott had talked about writing a Portland book, and that made running around and learning all the more fun. Eventually, in 2013, he convinced me to quit my job and write a book with him. Not being a writer myself, I had my doubts how I would contribute, but why not? I was turning 40 and wanted a life change. I loved the research side of it and since I was the one who lived in Portland I figured I could run around town looking for new oddities, dig through microfiche, take pictures, badger people for answers, and make the website.

So that's how this book came to be. We've had fun trying to make a unique guide that represents the things that we feel define Portland without covering all the usual travel-book tourist spots. We sure hope you enjoy it.

THANK YOU

Amidst all the PDX explorings that led to this book Aimee chanced-upon a bubbling drinking fountain at NE 57th and Sandy dedicated to the mysterious Chas. B. Merrick. Aimee dug up his obituary out of the *Oregonian*'s database and found out that, upon his untimely death, the city dedicated a fountain in his honor because he was an "Unusually useful as a citizen." Wow, *unusually useful*…hmph. That phrase caught our fancy and stayed with us throughout this entire guidebooking adventure. We even named an unusually useful fire stick after Chas B., just because it was soooo useful, and also made for fun limericks around the campfire. Anyhow, the result of all this is that we'd like to honor some of the websites and people that we think were unusually useful to us in the writing of *PDXccentric*. We'd like to bestow our own praise, in the form of…

Chas B. Merrick Unusual Usefulness Citation

Newspapers and Web:
> *Oregonian* digital archive hosted by the Mult.Co.Library
> *Willamette Week*, both paper and digital
> *Portland Mercury*, both paper and digital
> Café Unknown blog, written by Dan Haneckow
> Cyclotram blog, written by the mysterious brx0_
> History blogger Jeff Felker

In Person:
> **Aimee** would like to thank local ace historian Don Nelson for his help, willingness to share detailed files of information and friendly interest he took in her research, making her feel like she was a credible and able historian-in-the-making.
>
> **Scott** would like to thank Tom Murray, who owns the Hood River Artifacts used books and bad art shop, for his endless flow of ideas of PDX oddities to explore and his joyous enthusiasm for all things Portland.

In addition, there are, of course, innumerable people we owe thanks to who helped us in some way or another in our explorations. To try to thank everyone would inevitably leave others out, so instead we'd just like to express a group "Thank you" to anyone and everyone who remembers when we pestered you with questions.

We would like to thank some people by name would did meet with us in person and gave generously of their time to answer our never-ending slew of questions and perspective-gatherings. Among these are Dick Ponzi, Tres Shannon and Cat Daddy Pogson, Mary Priester, Merrill Denney, Terri Johnson, Wendy Gibson and Scott Wayne Indiana.

PDXccentric

An Odyssey of

PORTLAND

Oddities

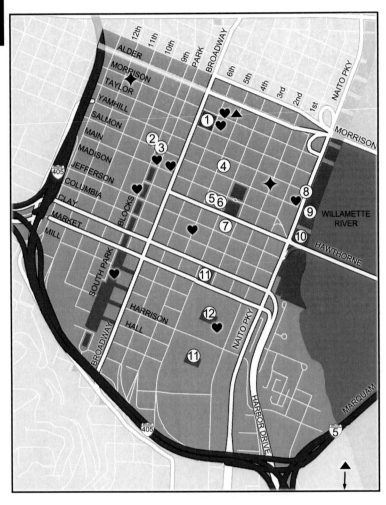

DOWNTOWN CORE – SOUTH

APPENDIX KEY

♥ Hot, Not, or Learn-a-lot Statues

◆ Custom Bike Racks

★ Intersection Murals

▲ Viewpoints

3

PC²

Where: SW 6th & Morrison

 45.519097 -122.679298

Nearby: Entry B9; App 1, #4-5;
App 2, #26; App 4, #5

MAP P. 2

OBSCURE — POPULAR
OBSCUR-O-METER

Pioneer Courthouse Square (PC²) has more secrets than you'd think, given it has been the most-visited spot in PDX since its gala 1984 opening. The design of the Square, chosen from a nationwide design competition (A12), is a collection of fun Post-Modernisms just like its 15-story older cousin just a few blocks to the south. Yup, the ever-popular PC² took many design inspirations from the just-completed and uber-controversial Michael Graves Portland Building (A6). Notice the columns, the keystone fountain, and the Portland Hotel gateway. As Square designers were once quoted in a 1999 *Willamette Week* article, they "out-Gravesed Graves" with their design flourishes. Seems that maybe Post-Modernism flourishes might go better with an outdoor civic playground than as a workplace.

<u>Echo Chamber:</u> The make-your-eyes-pop-open-in-surprise Echo Chamber is PC²'s neatest hidden feature. Well known to PDX'ers who were around for the 1984 gala opening of "Portland's Living Room," the Echo Chamber is virtually unknown to the other .618% of "new Portlandians" (more about .618 later). Go figure, but nowhere on or near the Echo Chamber does it tell you about its hidden ear-candy aural delight. When you find the small bricked half-amphitheater

under/next-to Starbucks, it's best to simply begin talking aloud to yourself as you approach the granite disk in its center…and once you stand exactly atop the engraved disk—oh-my-god WOW! You might feel a bit weird standing there talking to yourself, but nobody can hear you but yourself, look around and you'll probably see plenty of other sidewalk denizens talking to themselves—ha! If you're easily embarrassed, then hold up your cellphone and talk—as that's the kind of "normal crazy" we're all used to, like when you hear someone talking loudly to "themselves" in the grocery store.

Wanna know something even more secret about the Echo that even the PDX-in-the-know don't know? The Echo Chamber is a whisper gallery like over at Terry Schrunk (A7), but a better one. Try this: with two people, pick one of the circular curves with nobody sitting on it. One person talks "to" the seating curve while the other listens with their ear to the end of the curve. You'll "throw your voice" around the curve. Effing magic, huh!?! (If you're by yourself, set your phone down at one end of the curve, press play, and listen to your voicemail 'round the curve.)

Weather Machine: The Weather Machine provides Portland's <u>most entertaining two minutes of each day</u>, every day at noon. For the 99.7% of people who never even notice it, the Weather Machine is the globe-on-a-pole contraption between the Echo Chamber and VisCtr. Like so much of Portland, it was also designed via a public contest, this contest surprisingly won by BridgePort Brewing's founder Dick Ponzi. (B3) (App 5).

Here's what it does and why hardly anyone knows, unless you happen to be the kind of author geek who'll read the explanatory plaque twelve feet away on the Starbucks wall. Every day at noon trumpets blare a fanfare that can be heard for blocks around. Mist sprays out of the top as the globe displays its three charismatic weather talismans: Helia the Sunny, Blue Heron the Grey and Dragon the Stormy. After a brief showing of all three talismans, the day's weather-prediction pops up to reign over the square for the next 23:58.

Chicago's Allow Me

<u>Allow Me Statue:</u> Affectionately known as Umbrella Man, he was sculpted by controversial artist J. Seward Johnson. Little known is that he has almost-identical twins in Chicago and Philadelphia.

continued ➡

.618, The Golden Ratio: This is the decimal approximation of the Golden Ratio. Who knew that the design team behind PC^2 were Golden Ratio nutters who included divine-proportion spirals and Fibonacci sequences right under our unaware noses? The very center of the Square features a bronze sunflower manhole, mimicking the same 13/21 Fibonacci sunflower over at Sunnyside Piazza (E7). Also, adorning the top of every Starbucks metal column you'll see both the sunflower emblem as well as a Golden-ratio Nautilus-shell spiral. Who knew? And, even more bizarre to us Xccentrix is the fact that the Square's ramp in the brick

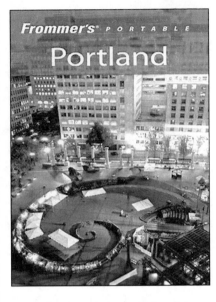

seating curves adheres to the curve of a Golden spiral arm. This epiphany first came to us when we saw an old *Frommer's* guide which showed an aerial photo of the Square when unknown booths/tents were set-up to spiral into the Square, just like a Nautilus. Further investigation up in the Square's office revealed a 1997 Festival of Flowers poster showing a flowered spiral and stating, "the spiral extends the geometry of the stair-ramp into the Square."

Design Contest: Downstairs in the hallway (to/from the Travel Portland info desk) is a fabulous display about the design competition for Pioneer Courthouse Square (A12). Many thanks to Randy Gragg for assembling the intriguing stories of how the Square came to be what it is. The display

Willard Martin's design model

posters detail how the winning Martin team created an actual wooden mock-up of their Square submission (now hidden in the OHS archives warehouse).

PIONEER COURTHOUSE SQUARE *PUZZLER*

From each of the following PC²-oriented numerical riddles, solve each one and the number you get corresponds to a letter in the alphabet. Turn these numbers into seven letters and unscramble the letters (with the help of the clue) into the word that solves the puzzler.

1. In the exact center of the square look for a circular bronze manhole disc representing the Golden Ratio spirals. Count the spiral arms circling one way, then count the reverse number of spiral arms (they should both be numerals in the Fibonacci sequence). Add the two. (As a back-up in case the manhole is covered, find the bronze Echo Chamber relief of "Square Construction" and add up the year numerals).

__ __ __ __ __ __ – __ __ __

2. Time of the hour hand on the Umbrella Man's watch. The exact time appears to be 8 minutes past this hour. __ __ __ __

3. In the Square's NW corner on the brick wall you'll find an honorary plaque (under a spirals medallion) showing name of the Square's Design Architect. Take the number of letters in his last name and subtract them from the number in his first name (this is also the number of his hats that are cast in commemorative bronze on the granite next to the keystone lecturn). __ __ __

4. Count the number of the standing white columns that border the north and south sides of the Square. Add the number of metal flowing faces in the Starbucks pavilion fountain, then subtract the number of umbrella-like glass/metal rain structures above the echo chamber.

__ __ __ __ __ __ __ __

5. On the east side of the Square is a milepost sign. Take Sapporo mileage, subtract Khabarovsk and then add the number of blocks to the waterfront. __ __ __ __ __ __ __ __ __

6. On the first series of the Echo Chamber's bronze bas-relief historic plaques, find "Francis Pettygrove" (Father of Portland). Add up the numerals in the date (it should be the same as the sum of the "Meier and Frank" in the third series.) __ __ __ __ __ __ __ __

7. On the Weather Machine count the number of red bulbs and subtract the number of blue bulbs from it. Add the number of octagonal tree planters at the SW corner of the Square. Subtract the number of chess pieces on the bronze chessboard overhanging the Echo Chamber.

__ __ __ __

A	B	C	D	E	F	G	H	I	J	K	L	M	N	O	P	Q	R	S	T	U	V	W	X	Y	Z
1	2	3	4	5	6	7	8	9	10	11	12	13	14	15	16	17	18	19	20	21	22	23	24	25	26

Assemble scrambled letters here: __ __ __ __ __ __ __
Answer Clue: "What Albert did to the speed of light?"

Answer: He __ __ __ __ __ __ __ __ it.

JUST ANOTHER FISH IN THE WALL

Where: 901 SW Salmon St (and 9th)

Google Coords ► 45.517815 -122.682231

Nearby: Entry A5; App 1, #8-10

A 2

MAP P. 2

OBSCUR-O-METER (OBSCURE — POPULAR)

This eye catching oh-so-photogenic sculpture resides adjacent to the NW corner of the South Park Blocks.

There's not much of a story behind this 11-foot Keith Jellum sculpture, except that people really like it. Moon Handbooks guidebook liked it enough to make it the cover of their comprehensive 2010 PDX guidebook.

ALL IN ALL, A GREAT
FISH IN THE WALL.

MOON HANDBOOKS

PORTLAND

8

Other than now having a fish in its wall, this corner has hosted some interesting bits of PDX restaurant history before Southpark Seafood arrived in 1998. In the early 1980s the Bhagwan's Rajneeshees operated a short-lived *Zorba the Buddha* discotheque on the corner, followed a few years later by the Widmer Brothers' first-ever brewpub. The Widmers partnered with the Heathman Hotel from '88 to '98 to run a brewpub/bakery/restaurant called *B. Moloch*. *B. Moloch* was Portland's first downtown upscale brewpub.

CURIOUSER? B. Moloch was a late 1800s French political cartoonist. Around the bar at Southpark Seafood you can still see some oversized B. Moloch art left over from back in the day. B. Moloch's Widmer sign can be seen in *Brainsmasher* (F11)

A 3

SIMON SAYS...

Where: The north end of the South Park Blocks at Salmon St. between Park & 9th

Google Coords ▶ **45.517623 -122.681980**

Nearby: Entry A5; App 1, #8-10

MAP P. 2

OBSCUR-O-METER
OBSCURE · POPULAR

"No one has the right to die and not leave something to the public and for the public good." —S. Benson

So started Portland's 100-year love affair with Simon Benson's "Benson Bubbler" drinking fountains. Simon Benson was a zillionaire self-made local timber tycoon, temperance advocate, and celebrated Portland philanthropist. In 1912 he donated the original 20 bubblers to the city. His stated intent was that city workers wouldn't have to resort to a saloon to slake their workday thirsts. Simon said, "I came to the conclusion that if a workman could get a drink of cold pure water on a street corner, without

TWENTY FOUNTAINS PRESENTED TO CITY
Gift of S. Benson, Millionaire

Oregonian 4-12-1912

Oregon Historical Society photo

obligation, he probably wouldn't go to a saloon so often…Such things work better for citizenship." (From *Simon Benson NW Lumber King* page 105). Thus, for 102 years now these Benson benefactions have freely bubbled a boisterous flow of Bull Run water, making them one of Portland's best-loved and recognizable icons.

Bubbler Xccentricities

1. There are now 52 official four-bowled Benson Bubblers, but only the 20 original ones have a curved plaque below the bowls stating "Presented by S. Benson 1912"

2. A woman named Nellie Robinson donated an additional 3 bubblers to the original 20 in 1921. Two of her bubblers are in front of Keller Auditorium and each has a circular badge atop its column celebrating

her gift. The third of her three is the city's sole three-bowled official "Benson Bubbler".

It's located in Ankeny Square directly on Naito Parkway. On the three "Nellies" all the bowls have some ornamental flourish, setting them apart from Simon's smooth-lipped bowls.

Nellie Robinson badge

3. There are only two official Benson Bubblers in the world not located in Portland. Maryhill Museum and Sapporo Japan.

4. Were it not for 1950s citizen hero Francis J. Murnane, we might not have any bubblers left on our streets. And, were it not for good citizen Dan Haneckow and his superb everything-Portland blog "Café Unknown," we here at Xccentral wouldn't have known about Murnane's one-man fight to save the Benson Bubblers. Huzzah Francis, and bravo Dan. Google them or click on links on our website.

Simon Benson memorial plaque

5. The funnest thing to do with a bubbler isn't to drink from it, but rather to hold your thumbs over the spouts to make them squirt. PDXtra points for style if you can squirt the memorial Simon Benson plaque from the bubbler at the North end of the South Park blocks (SW 9th and Salmon, near the Fish in the Wall, entry A2). Also, on a super-hot summer day, every Bubbler can become a mini playful mist-spraying cool-off fountain if you're good with your thumbs—never mind the Bollards, here's the Bubblers! (A9)

CURIOUSER? Hollywood doesn't seem clued-in as to just how cool our Bubblers are. Yeesh, Bubbler cameos are rarer than either Burnside Skatepark or Pittock Mansion. Alas, but the few Bubblers that have made it to the big screen are oh so fine. Huge props for Gus having Matt Dillon take a big Bubbler gulp in the first scene of *Drugstore Cowboy* (F4). Then, in 1990, the good-guy kung-fu cop in *Ironheart* (F9) takes a slurp as he surveys Milverstead's evil henchmen. And lastly, in *The Hunted*, (F15) TL Jones scampers past a Bubbler in hot pursuit of BD Toro.

QUEST

Where: 900 SW 5th Ave.

 45.517145 -122.678159

Nearby: App 1, #8; App 2, #25

OBSCURE POPULAR
OBSCUR-O-METER

Since its 1970 unveiling, when a group of young Rose Parade Princesses were shocked into silence when they pulled the cords to lift a drape off of the mammoth new sculpture, Quest has continued to cause many a double-take among casual 5th Ave. pedestrians.

Quest, chiseled out of the largest block of white marble ever quarried in modern times—a 190 ton single block—makes pretty much everyone question what exactly sculptor Alexander Von Svoboda had in mind with these entangled nude bodies. He claimed his inspiration from Michelangelo, chiseling at the magnificent white marble in an effort to "represent man's eternal search for brotherhood and enlightenment." Um, yeah, he must have been partaking in the Summer of Love perhaps. He had unearthed the largest hunk of pure white marble

Marble Block

in thousands of years…and he sculpted this out of it? Hmmmm, after he found his marble, did he then maybe lose his marbles??

Another funny thing about Quest is the affectionate nickname it has had since the 1980s—"Three Groins in the Fountain." Everyone from art critics to the *Oregonian* to Chuck Palahniuk has referenced this nickname.

But...but...but, the fountain clearly depicts four groins, with the Mark Zuckerberg look-alike guy elbowing out the 5th groin in his obvious search for enlightenment. Count 'em—four groins—two babes, one baby, and Mark. Did anybody actually look before coining the nickname? OK, OK...I guess "Four Groins in the Fountain" wouldn't make an apropos pun on the famous Sinatra song/movie *Three Coins in the Fountain*, would it? (And you know by now the PDXccentric loves puns).

The other popular nickname for Quest is "Family Night at the Y," maybe due to the baby on the fountain's backside (backside's got baby). But wow, we've never been to any YMCA where everyone cavorts naked together like that in any "eternal search for brotherhood." That must be the exciting YMCA the Village People were singing about. Sign us up.

The Count at work on clay model

CURIOUSER? For a photo-montage of the making of Quest, check wwww.alexvansvoboda.com, click the AMERICA tab, then click PROJECTS, and Quest. Also check www. healthheritageresearch.com/alexvonsvoboda for a Svoboda bio with photos.
YouTube Sinatra's *Three Coins in the Fountain*, about Rome's Trevi Fountain.

MINIATURE PORTLANDIAS

Where: 1120 SW 5th Ave

 45.515774 -122.679037

Nearby: App 2, #25

OBSCUR-O-METER

Scattered around downtown PDX, within a few blocks of the Portland Building, are a surprising assortment of miniature Portlandia statues. We say "surprising" because, first off, a majority of present-day Portlanders have never seen the namesake 40-foot statue…often thinking "Portlandia" is some sort of 4-year-old TV comedy starring the woman who was in the punk band that wrote *Light Rail Coyote* (D11). And secondly, most people have no idea that there are <u>any</u> miniature Portlandias, often thinking that the sculptor Kaskey never sold anything with the likeness of Portlandia on it.

Come take a little tour. Big Portlandia can seem a little aloof up on her perch, but when you see the miniatures up close and personal, you, like us, may find a newfound affection for Portlandia.

From Graves' design model

The Portland Building at 1100 SW 5th Ave. The best way to see Portlandia for the first time is from across the street so you can see her above the pesky trees. Once inside look up to see an enlarged City Seal emblem featuring Lady Commerce, aka Portlandia. Upstairs from the lobby is an art gallery displaying a 4-foot plaster Portlandia as well as a bunch of Portlandia memorabilia. Past the second-floor elevators you'll find the miniature model Portland Building on which architect Graves first crafted a micro-statue that he christened "Portlandia" for the Portland Building design contest.

Wells Fargo Building at 1300 SW 5th Ave. In the lobby arcade of the building, by the elevators, you'll see one of the four-foot bronze mini-Portlandias that have been cast and sold. Sculptor Kaskey commissioned a set of 12 of these 4-foot replicas, but to date only four of the series have been bought and created.

Heathman Hotel at 1001 SW Broadway. Upstairs in the second-floor library area is an 8-inch micro-replica of Portlandia. The Heathman's micro is one of five made originally to advertise a limited-edition run of 500 that were to be made and sold. After Portlandia arrived in Portland in Oct. 1985, micro-replicas like this were advertised in the *Oregonian*, selling for $695 in 1985. It took until 2010 to finally sell all 500 of these micro-replicas. To our knowledge, this one at the Heathman is the only micro on public display.

8" micro Portlandia

World Trade Center Building on Naito Parkway and Salmon Street. A four-foot Portlandia resides in a glass entryway, visible from the street and accessible inside the open door. This is your best chance to touch and fondle Portlandia, as there's nobody ever around in this hidden-away location. Extra neat is going up the steps to look down on her from above!

Pioneer Place at 710 SW 5th Ave. Atop Pioneer Place is a weathervane showing Lady Commerce holding her trident just like on the City Seal. This isn't quite Portlandia, but it's fun to see and point out nonetheless.

CURIOUSER? So far we've pointed out two of the four 4-foot replicas. For the other two; the first that was cast (*1/12* inscribed by her knee) is inside the front door at the Kaiser Permanente offices at 500 NE Multnomah (near Lloyd Ctr). The #4/12 replica was gifted to our sister city Sapporo and she resides in the outdoor Sapporo Art Park (our website has photos).

THE PORTLAND BUILDING

Where: 1120 SW 5th

⊕ **Google Coords** ▶ 45.515774 -122.679037

Nearby: App 2, #25; App1 #8

OBSCUR-O-METER

MAP P. 2

A 6

Or......*how I learned to stop worrying and dig Graves*. Graves, as in Michael Graves, the storied architect behind our world-famous Portland Building. The Portland Building is, no doubt about it, controversial. You could say Portland has a Strangelove/hate relationship with it, given that it was even controversial before being built and is still controversial these 33 years later. We LOVE the building, mainly for its eccentricity and the many-layered story behind both the architecture and the embattled icon that crouches above the front door. But since we're guidebook authors and our job is to point out things to see, we'll not go into our opinions about the Portland Building's place in architectural history and such. There are brilliant write-ups by better thinkers than us and we'll link you to them on our website. But, in brief, we've learned to stop worrying and dig Graves. Too bad Mayor Ivancie was so cheap...look how happy Louisville is with its Humana Building!

5 reasons to visit the Portland Building

1. Enter the front door below our beloved copper goddess *Portlandia*, just as Madonna appeared to do during *Portlandia*'s first Hollywood appearance in *Body of Evidence*. (F6)

   If it's drizzling you might get lucky enough to catch a drip of water on your tongue from *Portlandia*'s outstretched finger.

2. Inside the lobby the first thing you'll see, high up, is an enlarged City Seal. The City Seal is where architect Graves found his inspiration for *Portlandia*—a monumental personification of the Seal's Lady Commerce figure. Also in the lobby notice the free-standing shelf units which harken to Graves' original artistic tea set that he designed for Alessi back in 1980. In addition, on info-czar David Muir's desk look for the rare Portland Building cookie tin that was sold by Meier & Frank back in the early '80s.

Tin on David's desk

Alessi Tea Set

3. Head up the stairs to the second floor art atrium where you'll find all sorts of Portlandia arcana and much more. The 4-foot plaster miniature of Portlandia is one of four miniatures of that size you can see around town (A5).

4. In the hallway past the second floor atrium you'll find the actual glass-enclosed miniature of the Portland Building that Michael Graves submitted to the building design competition back in 1980. On the miniature you can see Graves' suggestive rendition of his "Portlandia Statue" concept (holding both trident and wreath of wheat). Also note the flamboyant garlands that had to be scaled-back on the actual building.

Graves' design model

5. The Hidden City. In the same hallway as above, you'll see a door for Meeting Room C. Behind that door hides our favorite PDXccentric secret—an entire miniature downtown Portland hand-crafted out of wood. No way! The mini-city dates back to 1971. One inch represents 50 feet, and thus every downtown block is 4 inches square. (Note: the meeting room is open to the public but sometimes there are actual meetings going on so you can't go in and play with the toy city.) The details are exquisite! Look for the exact mini-replicas of Pioneer Courthouse Square, Keller Fountain, Portland Building, Schrunk Plaza, Big Pink….and so much more. So fun!

The mini city's Pioneer Courthouse Square

TERRY SCHRUNK "WHISPER GALLERY"

Where: SW 4th & Madison

⊕ Google Coords ▶ 45.514756 -122.677797

Nearby: Appl #8

OBSCUR-O-METER

Terry Schrunk Plaza has a secret. Come close and lemme whisper it to you.

In this Federal-Park-built-atop-a-parking-garage you'll find a sunken circular amphitheater. The amphitheater, with its curved and stepped seating, looks like Pioneer Courthouse Square's Echo Chamber. Get it? Yup, this is an echo chamber that's even less-known than the little-publicized PCS Echo Chamber (A1). And, even better, this is an echo chamber-in-the-round. Go ahead and stand in the center and jabber away like the Occupy'rs did back in 2011 when they Occupied this park and made speeches where everyone would echo/repeat what was being said. Nowadays nobody will hear your echo but yourself. And you'll love it.

360° Echo!

Never heard of a "Whisper Gallery"?? Well, neither had we...until we had. London's St. Paul's Cathedral is famed, as is NYC's Grand Central Station. The Schrunk Amphitheater might not make any top-10 list, but it does work, at least a bit. Have a friend crouch down and whisper "to" the curving seat...while you put your ear to the same curve on the other side... and WOW, no way, the whisper travels the curve!

Xccentrics and/or homeless may think you're nutty as you giggle in whisper/echo awe, but be confident that you're probably less nutty and a whole lot more science-oriented than those mere pedestrians. If you're alone maybe bring up a tune on your smart phone and let it play and throw a whisper around the curve to yourself. Schrunk magic—who would have thought?

CURIOUSER? For other echo chamber/whisper galleries around town check out Council Crest, The Little Prince Sculpture near the Moda Center, the bowl at the Burnside Skatepark (E3) and, of course, Pioneer Courthouse Square.
This park had a cameo in the movie *The Hunted* (F15).

MILL ENDS
(The Beginnings of the Ends)

A
8

MAP P. 2

Where: SW Naito Parkway & Taylor

⊕ Google Coords ▶ **45.516199 -122.673234**

Nearby: App 1, #8; App 2, #25

OBSCURE · POPULAR
OBSCUR-O-METER

Mill Ends is Portland's claim-to-fame "World's Smallest Park," though puzzlingly, virtually everything written about the park has wrong/misleading info about the park's origins. More on that later though—let's first enjoy the park for what it is, before we delve into what it isn't.

Mill Ends is a manhole-sized park in the middle of the traffic median on Naito Parkway, just a block north of the Salmon Street Springs fountain. The quirky little park took its eccentric name from Dick Fagan's *Oregon Journal* column "Mill Ends." Dick was a jovial man-about-town and his popular and whimsical odds 'n' ends column was a grab bag of the day-to-day minutiae of city life—current events, famous people sightings, civic happenings, etc etc.

Is Mill Ends worth visiting just to see a manhole-sized garden with maybe a small tree in it? You betcha! A big part of the charm of Mill Ends is how the good citizens of PDX treat the park. Since the park's 1954 birth (more on that later) Portlanders have enjoyed sprucing up the park with a wide assortment of miniature adornments—from a famed miniature ferris wheel to random figurines, Xmas ornaments and St. Patty's Day greenery. Just as Joe Portland likes to knit bomb and attach toy horses to horse rings, etc…he/she/LGBT also likes to adorn Mill Ends. But since everything is in miniature, you'll have to actually stop in the crosswalk for an up-close inspection to see what can be seen.

OK, now some stuff about how our claim that everyone is wrong about the beginnings of Mill Ends. What "everyone" has correct is that Dick Fagan named the tiny park and sometimes (not often) wrote about a leprechaun who lived there. What everyone has wrong are the details of the park's origins. Mill Ends was not founded in 1948 as popularly reported, nor was it founded on St. Patrick's Day, nor did it have anything to do with leprechauns when it began.

After pouring over *Oregon Journal* archives it's clear that the park originated on Feb 23, 1954 as a publicity stunt. In early 1954 Portland was in an epic battle with the city of Columbus, Ohio over the title "City of Roses." Portland had been nationally known as the "The City of Roses" for half a century at that point, but Columbus had just put in the nation's largest rose garden and they were rose'd-up for a showdown. The battle was on

Oregon Journal 2-23-54

and PDX responded with city-wide rose plantings and declared Feb. 21-27, 1954 "Rose Planting Week," to rally the good citizens to rise up and rose-up the city.

One such effort, most likely the idea of Dick Fagan, was to plant a single rose bush in a hole in the traffic median outside his *Oregon Journal* office. City fathers gathered for a rose-planting photo-op around the hole in the traffic median with Dick Fagan (2/23/54). They dedicated the lightpost-hole "Envoy Park" after that year's test-rose winner the *Portland Envoy Rose* (no mention in print of either "Mill Ends" or leprechauns at this point). A week later (3/7) the *Journal* runs a photo of Fagan posing with City Commissioner Ormond Bean at Envoy Park, stating the men were tussling over the park's name, Fagan lobbying to name the "World's Smallest Park" after his column. The next week (3/15) the park once again graced the *Journal*'s Features

'Envoy,' 'Mill Ends'—Which One?

Oregon Journal 3-7-54

Fagan

Oregon Journal 3-15-54

page and apparently Fagan's backroom horse-trading won him the day, as the park was then called Mill Ends for the first time in print, showing a photo of Fagan prepping the park for some St. Patty's Day snail races. Two days later (3/17) Fagan once again rallies another photo-op for Mill Ends Park when the "First Annual St. Patrick's Day Classic" snail races were held in the now so-named "Mill Ends, the World's Smallest Park." Thus, the legendary park was actually born 6 years after the urban-mythic beginning of the Ends that most popular literature states (like the *Guinness Book of Records*, which upon granting Mill Ends its "World's Smallest" title in 1971, commented, "…was designated in 1948 at the behest of the city journalist Dick Fagan…").

SALMON STREET SPRINGS FOUNTAIN

Where: Naito Parkway & Salmon St.

 Coords ▶ 45.515369 -122.673278

Nearby: App 1, #8; App 2, #25;
Entry E5

OBSCURE — POPULAR
OBSCUR-O-METER

The SSSF is the funnest fountain park/ plaza in Portland, kind of like the fun backyard sprinkler you played in as a kid. Even better, this fountain isn't tucked into a shady downtown skyscraper block—it's right in Portland's sunny front yard, the Waterfront

Misters, it's great for kids!

Park. Yippee! This fountain is meant to play in, so bring a swimsuit & towel (there are nearby bathrooms to change in).

This being weird Portland, of course the SSSF has its odd eccentricities. The first is that the fountain's name came from another PDX naming contest (A12). SSSF won-out over other such nuggets as Waltzing Waters, Pump

Wedding Cake

and Circumstance, H2Ohhhh, Noah's Arc, Old Facefull, Geezers Geysers, and Spurts Illustrated. More Xccentric though than the SSSF naming is the street-side mounted plaque that describes the 3 squirt-cycles that the fountain sequences through. (20 minutes each sequence, with a 30 sec lag in-between). Strangely, this plaque suggests that these cycles somehow represent day-to-day Portland:

"Salmon Street Springs was designed to celebrate city life and urban rhythms. The continuous play of water from early morning until after midnight reflects daily life in the city. Changing water patterns herald the day's beginning; morning, noon, and evening rush hours; night life; and midnight, the symbolic end of the day."

What kinda nonsense is that? Who won the contest to make up the nonsense on the plaque? Anyhow, the fountain's three cycles are nicknamed Misters, Wedding Cake, and Bollards. Misters and Wedding Cake look somewhat like their names...but Bollards...huh? Why did the

most exciting squirt get the lamest name? Hell, why didn't they just call it Bollocks instead? No wait…never mind the Bollocks, call it Sex Pistols!!

All humor aside (yeah right), as the plaque describes in its quasi-poetic jumble of words, the 3 cycles somehow relate to "heralding the day" and some quizzical mumbo-jumbo about all-day rush hours. Huh? Hmmmm?

Besides being fun to play in, photographers also love the SSSF. Near dusk when the fountain evidently cycles to "symbolically end the day" photo pros can tighten their apertures to nicely capture some ethereal blur. **On a sunny day** (yeah right) **Misters puts on the best show**, but only for people in the know. With the sun directly at your back walk towards the sprinkly edge of Misters and as you feel the spray "heralding your day", <u>Whoa</u>, at first one rainbow will encircle you, then possibly two! Get your friend and smartphone and quicker than you can say, "New Facebook Profile Pic" you'll have a rainbow'd reason to "celebrate city life."

CURIOUSER? More newspaper contest name articles listed on our website.

This fountain can be seen briefly in movies: *Down and Out with the Dolls* (F14), *Brainsmasher* (F11), *Hear No Evil* (F10) and *Free Willy* (F7).

UNPAVING PARADISE

Where: The west side Portland waterfront from the Hawthorne Bridge to Steel Bridge

Google Coords ▶ ------------------

Nearby: Entry E5; App 1, #13

A10

MAP P. 2

OBSCUR-O-METER

In July 1970 Joni Mitchell sang in her hit song *Big Yellow Taxi*, "They paved paradise and put up a parking lot." Back then that was how America was going...but not in Portland.

"Don't it always seem to go,
That you don't know what you've got 'til it's gone..."

Beginning in mid-1969, a group of citizens banded together to suggest that Portland do just the opposite—unpave in order to create a paradise. The issue was Harbor Drive, the waterfront freeway stretching along the downtown side of the Willamette River. The State Highway Dept. officials, circa 1969, were inclined to widen the existing waterfront freeway. Instead of shouting a "hooray" for quickened commutes, a citizen group formed and enlisted legendary maverick governor Tom McCall in the call for creating a park along the Willamette instead of an enlarged freeway. The building of the I-405 bypass freeway was underway, raising the question, "Why do we need a riverfront freeway if we'll soon have Fremont Bridge and a downtown bypass freeway?" In hindsight we now might say "good thinking," but most cities in that era didn't foster "good thinking," but rather thinking that leaned towards more freeways and faster suburban commutes. Portland citizens didn't think that way and neither did Governor McCall. Miracle of miracles, after four years of citizen participation in pro-active politics, Portland was on its way in 1974 to having a riverfront park and esplanade instead of a redundant freeway.

Other cities have been jealous of Portland for 40 years. The citizens had a good idea, the mayor bought-in, the governor bought in…shit got undone and good got done. This Portland event is now a milestone in national urban-planning annals, being the first major freeway in America to be intentionally removed. "When Portland decided to tear down the Harbor Drive freeway, the city made one of the key decisions that transformed it into a national model for effective city planning."* (PreserveNet.com)

> *"Don't it always seem to go,*
> *That you don't know what you've got 'til it's gone,*
> *They paved paradise,*
> *And put up a parking lot"*

Not here…not in Portland.

2014

From the Burnside Bridge

Nowadays, most all that's left of Harbor Drive are the two clover-leaf bikeways that descend from the Hawthorne Bridge down to the Waterfront Park, as well as a ghost-ramp stub where the Steel Bridge ramped-down to Harbor Drive (E5).

BUT, if you want somewhere unique to sit down and wax nostalgic about one of Portland's milestone urban-planning successes, then look to Couch Park up in NW at Glisan and 19th. Strangely enough and known to almost nobody, the city re-purposed the torn-up cement bits of Harbor Drive into the walls around the park and a seating area on the park's grassy knoll. Go visit old Harbor Drive, have a seat and maybe sing a little song about how we unpaved some paradise.

> **Concrete chunks dug out of Harbor Drive are being used to make a 120-foot "rubble wall" in Couch Park.**
>
> *Oregonian 9-12-77*

CURIOUSER? *From The Preservation Institute online write-up about Harbor Drive, A MUST-READ at http://www.preservenet.com/freeways/FreewaysHarbor.html.

Also Google "CNU Harbor Drive" for a succinct write-up.

On our website we have the *Oregonian* article about the re-purposing at Couch Park, as well as numerous historic photos of Harbor Drive.

LOVEJOY AND KELLER FOUNTAIN PLAZAS

Where: Lovejoy: SW 3rd & Harrison
Keller: SW 4th & Clay

Google Coords ► **L: 45.509348 -122.679932**
K: 45.512660 -122.678832

Nearby: App 1, #14

OBSCUR-O-METER

The Lovejoy and Keller fountain park-plazas were born of the same visionary father, famed landscape architect Lawrence Halprin. These siblings were the first-born of Portland's now-numerous square-block fountain parks. Both were designed and constructed in the late 1960s.

The 1960s in Portland was a time of civic soul-searching. Downtown was dying. The suburbs were winning. A big Re-Think was needed. Surprisingly (at least compared to cities that flubbed), Portland righted its sinking ship. Politicians and the public opted for some tough-love and enacted the city's first Urban Renewal District (South Auditorium). This was the entire south end of the downtown core. Basically, the city wiped the decaying urban area clean and said, "Let's start over." In hindsight, the plan, like all too many Urban Renewals, didn't achieve all its goals, but the HUGE SUCCESS of the plan was a string of interconnected parks, most notably the Lovejoy and Forecourt (Keller) Fountain plazas. Upon their completion NYC architecture critic Ada Louise Huxtable praised them as, "one of the most important urban spaces since the Renaissance" (*NY Times*, 6/21/1970). High praise indeed! As Portland's own Randy Gragg

Lovejoy

Oregonian 9-25-66

'Here Is One Acre Of Pure Pleasure'

Portland City Archives

adroitly points out in his exquisite book *Where the Revolution Began*, these fountains laid the participatory and playful groundwork for all of Portland's subsequent urban-planning winners such as Waterfront Park, Pioneer Courthouse Square, Jamison Square, etc.

Nowadays these two parks aren't nearly as "successful" (i. e. crowded) as the other just-named plazas, but therein lies their charm. No tourist hordes, no overwhelm of screaming kids, no raucous events...just a peaceful urban oasis. Wonderfully, each plaza has enough nooks and soothing waterfall noise to offer some respite and peace from Portland's successfully busy downtown-a-go-go.

Lovejoy Fountain

Popsicle sticks

The Lovejoy fountain isn't nearly as popular as its better-looking younger sibling, but it's our favorite of the two, especially for its relative solitude. Here's a couple of other reasons to feel the love:

<u>First</u>, the Lovejoy reminds us of the cascades that were once on the Columbia River before The Dalles Dam flooded-over them in 1957, namely Celilo Falls. Lovejoy not only mimics the falls, but also the downriver channels which spawned The Dalles' odd name. Early 1800s French trappers called the myriad of rocky river channels *Les Dalles of the Columbia*, "dalles" roughly translating as flagstone-like rock channels. The Lovejoy mimics the now-underwater channels, like "Les Dalles of the Lovejoy."

<u>Second</u>, the Lovejoy is the best fountain in the city for stick races. Sweet—nothing's better than a death race at the Lovejoy with a 22 on the line! Any local twig will do, but popsicle sticks are more fun because not only do you get to eat the ice cream off them in preparation, but you also can name or adorn your personal watercraft for added float-karma and Gusto. Believe us, if your stick floats woefully

continued ➡

behind that of your bitter rival, you'll have wished you had adorned it with encouraging flourish. ANYHOW, hurl your crafts into the upper bubbler pool and then madly yell encouragement as you scamper around the falls to cheer on your champion. Whoever makes it into the "Big Eddy" whirlpool-of-death first wins. Loser chugs, and buys…of course (best to use plastic cups on/around the cement plaza to decrease your chance of authorities coming along to ruin your fun).

Keller Fountain

The Keller is a square block of tree-rimmed gurgling waterfalls and pools inviting you to dip your feet, legs and maybe even whole selfs. Like the hokey-pokey sings, *you put your whole self in, you put your whole self out, you put your whole self in and you shake it all about…blah blah blah… that's what it's all about.* Yup, the Hokey-Pokey is what Keller is all about. The genius of Lawrence Halprin is that he dared to design fountains that inspired PLAY. Traditional plaza fountains, like the Trevi in Rome or the Buckingham in Chicago are not for hokey-pokeying…are NOT for PLAYING IN. Just look, don't enter!

Not in Portland. Halprin, bless his hippy heart, eschewed that tired ethic and designed his fountains to be intentionally interactive and inviting—just like a waterfall swimming-hole in nature. The Keller Fountain is exactly this—an urban waterfall swimming-hole that begs you to put your whole self in. It begs you to scamper and jump the channels and walk the ledges and simply frolic. And yeah, don't miss the hidden dry nook behind the waterfall curtain! Thanks Larry, you set a great example here in Portland for the rest of the world to follow. We owe you!

Ira Keller Fountain

28

Opening day June '70

Portland City Archives

CURIOUSER? Check out the movie *The Hunted* (F15) where Tommy Lee Jones tracks Benicio Del Toro behind the waterfall of the Keller Fountain. The Lovejoy Fountain was featured in *Jackass* Season 1 "Urban Kayaking" (link on our website).

PORTLAND, CONTESTED

Where: SW Montgomery between 2nd & 3rd

⊕ Google Coords ▶ 45.510759 -122.678667

Nearby: App 1, #14

MAP P. 2

OBSCURE · POPULAR

OBSCUR-O-METER

Portland seems to like naming and designing stuff via contests and competitions, all starting back in 1845 with the original coin-flip that named the city. Here are a bunch of our Xccentric favorites, ordered by date.

We've placed this entry here at Pettygrove Park, because it is one of the "decided-by-contest" locations and also has a plaque commemorating the original coin-flip.

Coin-flip. In 1845 city founders Asa Lovejoy and Francis Pettygrove decided to flip a coin to decide whether the name of the new city should be Boston or Portland. They flipped Pettygrove's oversized 1835 penny that he had carried west with him from Maine. The story of the flip has been told many different ways, but it seems they each flipped three times and whoever got the most heads out of their three flips would win. Pettygrove won and Portland it is.

The single best research we've ever read about this famed flip is on Dan Haneckow's exemplary *Café Unknown* blog, titled "The Vexed Question, Portland or Boston?"

"Heads it's Portland ⸱⸱
    Tails it's Boston" ⸱⸱
the flip of a coin named Portland in 1845

1835 penny

2007 penny

Now America's 14ᵗʰ Port · Her 22ⁿᵈ City

Lovejoy vs. Pettygrove Revisited. In 1966, as the South Auditorium Renewal District took shape, the city had to decide which of Halprin's new park plazas to name Lovejoy and which Pettygrove (A11). Voilá, out of the Historical Society came the actual historic 1835 penny that

Oregonian 7-27-1966

1835 COPPER PENNY, used 121 years ago in naming of Portland, was retrieved from Oregon Historical Society and used Tuesday in naming of parks.

Lovejoy and Pettygrove had flipped in 1845 to name the new city of Portland. Mayor Schrunk flipped and this time Lovejoy won. (Newspaper articles on our website.)

WORLD PORT OF THE PACIFIC
RED
WHITE
GREEN
GOLD
CITY OF ROSES

PRESENTATION to City Council this week by Commercial Club of Portland of above proposed design for an official city flag has raised question about status of two designs received earlier. The council has not yet taken any action on proposal made by Commercial Club.

BLUE SILK
GOLD
BLACK
1851
VARIOUS COLORS
GOLD FRINGE

FLAG IN sketch above was donated to City Council in 1929 by Portland Lang Syne Society, but design never was officially adopted. Double thickness and intricate needlework pushed cost to $172 per copy. This flag hangs from staff on stand in council chamber at City Hall.

WHITE
RED
BLUE-GREEN

CITY COUNCIL accepted above design and awarded $25 prize to Portlander H. W. Frederick in 1917. Horizontal stripe is intended to represent Willamette River, with solid red circle symbolizing City of Portland. All sketches are by John Waddingham, art director for The Oregonian.

Oregonian 4-5-1969

Portland Flag. Only a minority of Portlanders know that the city has an official flag (E1). Even fewer know that the flag was designed via a 1969 contest and has since been redesigned into today's version. Even fewer fewer people, even amongst vexillophiles, know that Portland has had a century of city flags designed via various contests. See website for *Oregonian* articles, photos, links, etc.

Expose Yourself to Art. Photographer/journalist Mike Ryerson and pub-owner future-mayor Bud Clark teamed up to craft this image for a "Zap the Clap" venereal disease prevention campaign. After taking the photo, Ryerson ran a contest in his neighborhood newspaper to caption the photo. Ryerson especially liked "Wanna buy a watch?", but "Expose Yourself to Art" won out. The poster is now one of the most-famed in the entire world. Read Ryerson's personal account on the poster printer/copyright holder's website: www.ErrolGraphics.com.

Pioneer Courthouse Square. In 1980 the Portland Development Commission staged an international competition for the design of the Square. The Commission received an astounding 162 entries which a citizen committee then whittled to five finalists. The finalists erected miniature mock-ups of their designs and Willard Martin's team won-out (photos on our website or Entry A1). However, after the Martin team's

continued ➡

design was chosen the Square was almost never built due to lack of funding and Mayor Ivancie's rancor. The "rest of the story" is a fascinating one with the PDX citizens coming to the rescue and the parking lot being painted a crazy orange. Check www.TheSquarePdx.org (About us/history tab), or links on our website.

Portland Building. The Portland Building (A6) is the result of a still-controversial design competition held in early 1980. The Michael Graves design was one of three finalists, the other two being more of the glass-box variety of office building. Needless to say, the colorful building has earned heaps of

Oregonian 2-8-1980

both ridicule and praise for the past 30 years, but the one sure thing it did was put Portland "on the architectural map" as well as on the pages and covers of national magazines.

Oregon Journal 4-22-1982

Much has been written about the building…and on our website we link to some of our favorite commentaries as well as hosting the pages of the *Oregonian* that detail the design contest as it played out in 1980.

***Portlandia* Statue.** *Portlandia* was envisioned by Portland Building architect Graves as a monumental personification of the City Seal's Lady Commerce figure. A national design competition ensued for the sculpture commission and over 100 entries were pared-down to five. These five were asked to submit models of their proposed sculptures. Raymond Kaskey's windblown crouching goddess won. History has pretty much forgotten about the four other semi-finalists…but don't worry, we found them and have them on our website for you to judge them for yourselves. (Also check Appendix 6 for our take on the *Portlandia* saga.)

Weather Machine. The Weather Machine was an original design element of Pioneer Courthouse Square, but it took an extra four years to figure out what the machine should look like. A design contest was run, 40 international entries were received, and curiously enough the winning submission was from BridgePort Brewery's Dick Ponzi and his team. Willard Scott came out from *The Today Show* to christen the machine on 8/24/88 to a gala standing-room crowd in the Square. Newspaper articles are on our website.

Will's whimsical weather machine

The machine, designed by the late Portland architect Will Martin, would feature mechanical people ringing bells and one who would spill rainwater on the heads of the unwary.

Oregonian 12-8-1985

Salmon Street Springs Fountain. (A9). This fountain was named via a 1989 *Oregonian* naming contest. Ideas poured in: *H2Ohhhh, Splashes of Laughter Friendship Fountain, Let Us Spray,* and *Noah's Arc*...to name just a few. Hahahaha...read the rest in the *Oregonian* articles on our website.

Bud Clark Limerick. "Whoop whoop was the curious cheer of a colorful barkeep near here...." See entry C7 for the sidewalk-engraving contest dedicated to our favorite mayor.

Tilikum Crossing Bridge. In 2013 Tri-Met held a contest to name its new light-rail/pedestrian bridge. The contest elicited nearly 9,500 entries, the most popular being "Working Kirk Reeves." Working Kirk was a well-loved trumpeting street performer who tragically died in 2012. Prior to the Tri-Met contest, Mayor Sam Adams had declared 11/18/2013 "Kirk Reeves Day" in Portland. The eccentric citizen effort to name the bridge after Working Kirk eventually failed but Kirk's memory lives on in Wikipedia, Facebook, Google, and a 2014 building mural at Grand and Lloyd.

And one more....

Portland Cream Doughnut. In the naming of this famed Voodoo Doughnut (B11), Portland won-out over Boston again, just like back in 1845 for the original coin-flip naming of Portland. This time though Tres and Cat Daddy crafted an ingenious win for Portland when they took a typical Boston Cream Donut and added two eyes to it because, "unlike Boston, Portland has vision." Huzzah, Portland beats Boston again, this time thanks to some Voodoo juju. Nyah nyah nyah Boston... come visit, but please don't stay. 😊

33

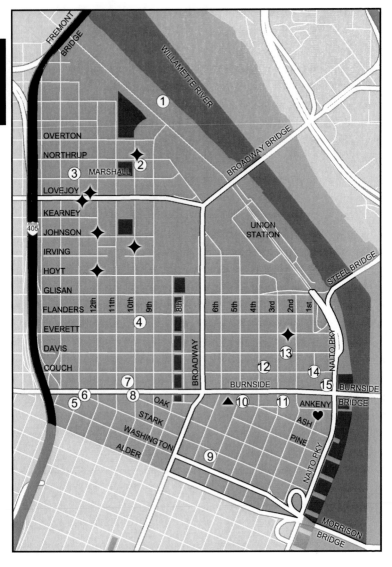

OVERTON

NORTHRUP

MARSHALL

LOVEJOY

KEARNEY

405

JOHNSON

IRVING

HOYT

GLISAN

FLANDERS

EVERETT

DAVIS

COUCH

FREMONT BRIDGE

WILLAMETTE RIVER

BROADWAY BRIDGE

UNION STATION

STEEL BRIDGE

12th 11th 10th 9th 8th

6th 5th 4th 3rd 2nd 1st

BROADWAY

BURNSIDE

NAITO PKY

BURNSIDE BRIDGE

OAK

STARK

WASHINGTON

ALDER

ANKENY

ASH

PINE

NAITO PKY

MORRISON BRIDGE

DOWNTOWN CORE – NORTH

APPENDIX KEY

 Hot, Not, or Learn-a-lot Statues

 Custom Bike Racks

 Intersection Murals

 Viewpoints

TANNER CREEK

Where: Directly across the street from 1362 NW Naito Parkway at 9th

 45.533741 -122.679518

Nearby: App 2, #30

B1

MAP P. 34

OBSCURE — POPULAR

OBSCUR-O-METER

West Hills

Original Route of Tanner Creek

Willamette River

Couch Lake

Tanner Creek is buried alive beneath Portland. Tanner Creek in the 1850s was a free-flowing little stream meandering through W/NW Portland. The creek got its name from leather tanner Daniel Lownsdale who opened the West's first tannery along the creek at the site of present-day Providence Park. Fast forward to the 1880s and booming Portland hungered for more flat, buildable land. City fathers decided to bury Tanner Creek in its own brick-lined sewer pipe which would wind down from Goose Hollow, through Couch's Addition (Pearl), then empty, more or less, into the Willamette. Goodbye uneven creek lowlands, hello Union Station, Hoyt rail yards, Multnomah Field, warehouses etc, etc. Throughout the next century street run-off storm sewers were funneled into the Tanner pipe, basically making the former sylvan creek bed into a sewer expressway straight into the Willamette.

In most cities this might be the end of the story. Tanner Creek buried, paved-over and turned into a sewer pipe. Industrial progress wins. End of story. Not in Portland. In the late 1990s a huge project was begun to steer storm run-off away from Tanner's free-flow-to-the-Willamette. DEQ mandate said Portland had to treat storm run-off for pollutants, but it would allow the original flow of Tanner Creek to run treatment-free into the Willamette (part of the Big Pipe scheme). Ten years later and about a zillion dollars spent, Tanner Creek is now "alive" again in its own private pipe, though still buried. Buried alive... the flowing dead...a zombie creek!

Gravestone

36

Strangely, after Tanner's underground resurrection a mysterious faction of urban planners set out to commemorate the newly dead/alive creek. At the Kings Hill MAX station (at Providence Park) you can read an extensive engraving detailing the creek's storied history. Additionally, just north ("downstream") of the stadium in a housing tower plaza you'll find a massive engraved gravestone with a quote from *A River Runs Through It*. Hmmm, is this a Norm Maclean eulogy for a dead creek or a celebration of a resurrected zombie creek? Strangest of all are two engraved granite gravestones memorializing the buried creek embedded in the Pearl sidewalks on both Glisan and Flanders streets (both between 11th and 12th). These sidewalk gravestones say nothing more than "Tanner Creek"—no info, no plaque, no reason for their placement—just gravestones mounted over the buried-alive creek. Odd. Which other city places sidewalk gravestones over buried creekbeds?

Here at PDXccentral we love our Tanner

The creek's not dead to us, just hard to see and play with. Since Tanner's resurrection, the creek now flows free and "pure" until it spills out an outfall pipe as a one-foot waterfall into the Willamette. Yay, Tanner Creek Out-Falls! But, this only happens in summer/fall when the Willamette is low and not swamping the outfall pipe. Fun is that there's a manhole just 100 yards upstream of the outfalls where you can crouch down, eye-to-the-manhole, to

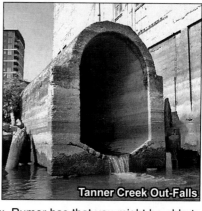

Tanner Creek Out-Falls

see/hear the trickling creek below. Rumor has that you might be able to drop two sticks down the manhole and into the creek for an 1850s-style race

Look and Listen

to the Willamette. Trouble though is the 10-foot-high Outfalls pipe is located on the riverbank behind/beside the Police Stables on Naito Pkwy (directly next to the derelict Centennial Mills building). So, how you'd actually get to the Outfall pipe to watch the sticks emerge is a question for you to ponder on your own. (The manhole is across Naito from the Police front door, between the RR and Naito. The manhole is a raised-up type—put your ear or eye to a hole and…Hello Tanner!)

NICE RACKS

Where: NW 10th and Northrup

 45.531459 -122.681256

Nearby: App 2, #28

See more racks in Appendix 2

OBSCURE — POPULAR

OBSCUR-O-METER

Portland's got some nice racks. Other cities have other kinds of racks that garner media attention, but no city sports as nice a set of racks as Portland. Bike racks, of course.

Portland, ever eccentric, just wasn't willing to settle for the ordinary "staple-style" bike rack, nor the improved "wave-style" model. Nope, Portland decided to support the racks of individual businesses who wanted to add some unique flare to their sidewalks. Businesses have loved the idea, instead of the usual staple-shaped bolt-on rack, they can get creative and design a rack that will lift and separate their location from that of their neighbor. A nice rack out front is a way for a business to turn

Petrich Store owner Tom and Merrill Denney with the first "art rack" installed in the US

heads and say *"look at me...notice me!"* Seems that an artful rack uplifts everyone's spirits.

The idea of artsy racks has now spread to cities far and wide, most notably to NYC where Talking Heads frontman David Byrne has designed a nice set of sidewalk bolt-ons. But wouldn't you know, artsy bike racks began here in Portland, or more specifically at a country store out in the wine country of SW PDX. True. Back in 1993 a cyclist/metalsmith, Merrill

David Byrne's rack

Denney, asked the owner of the Petrich Country Store why he didn't have a bike rack at his store. Tom, the owner replied, "Well, Merrill, you work with metal, why don't you make me one?" Whoa, sometimes a great notion just comes along! Merrill Denney got busy and crafted a handlebars 'n' wheel sort of rack, something different and unique that would suit the country store. Unfortunately the old country

Merrill's latest rack at Frock on NE Alberta

store burned to the ground and the rack Denney built for it wasn't installed until they rebuilt in 1996. Merrill took this same design to the chain of Bike and Hike stores and they bought one for each location, and the rest, as they say is history. Merrill Denney formed "Creative Metalworks" and for the past 20 years has been crafting custom racks all over Portland, as well as for other cities around the country. Nowadays PDX has so many nice racks that you could say our cup runneth over!

Sooo, we've decided to locate this entry in the Pearl because the Pearl has some of the nicest racks in all of Portland. Our Hollywood, just like in L.A., has plenty of nice racks too, but you'll have to turn to Appendix 2 to see the map and addresses of the racks we currently know of. But here in the Pearl, Merrill outdid himself by creating a marvelous rendition of the Fremont Bridge…and not only did he create five of them, no two are <u>exactly</u> alike. For geeks like us it's fun to bike to all five and make a list of the number of cars, SUV's, trucks and semis crossing the double deck spans to find the difference on each one.

Collect 'em all: There are two at NW 10th and Northrup, one on either side of NW Lovejoy between 11th and 12th and one on NW 10th near Irving St.

One of five Fremont Bridge bike racks

CURIOUSER? Check Appendix 2 for complete map and listings.

BEERGINNINGS

Where: 1313 NW Marshall St.

Google Coords 45.530837 -122.684557

Nearby: App 2, #28-30

B3

MAP P. 34

OBSCUR-O-METER

This entry is placed at BridgePort Brewery because BridgePort is the oldest operating microbrewery in Oregon, and also still in its original location. Within walking distance you can also see the original locations of Widmer and Portland Brewing. Check out Appendix 5 for a complete rundown of Portland's Beerginnings and to read the story of how it all began.

BridgePort Brewery: 1313 NW Marshall. Portland's Oldest Microbrewery....

The Portland Cordage Co.
Manufacturers of all kinds of Cordage.
Portland, Oregon.

But...Portland microbrewing all actually started with:

Cartwright Brewing Company: 617 SE Main. Oregon's First Microbrewery since Prohibition. 1980-1982

After Cartwright Brewery failed, the McMenamin Brothers purchased Cartwright's Barley Mill and installed it in a place of honor in their new (1983) *Barley Mill Pub* at 1629 SE Hawthorne.

The Cartwright's Mill

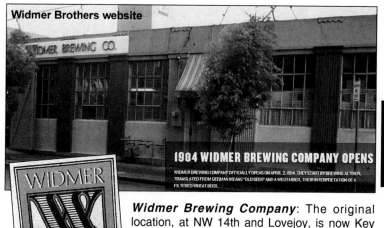

Widmer Brothers website

1984 WIDMER BREWING COMPANY OPENS

WIDMER BREWING COMPANY OFFICIALLY OPENS ON APRIL 2, 1984. THEY START BY BREWING ALTBIER. TRANSLATED FROM GERMAN MEANS "OLD BEER" AND A WEIZENBIER. THEIR INTERPRETATION OF A FILTERED WHEAT BEER.

Look, no "Brothers"

Widmer Brewing Company: The original location, at NW 14th and Lovejoy, is now Key Bank. Founded in April 1984, but didn't sell beer until April 1985.

McMenamin's Hillsdale Brewery & Public House: 1505 SW Sunset Blvd. Oregon's first brewpub since Prohibition. Served first brewpub beer November 1985.

Portland Brewing: The original location, at 14th and Flanders, is now is now Rogue Distillery and Public House.

41

LOVEJOY COLUMNS

Where: 320 NW 10th

Google Coords ▶ 45.525542 -122.681149

Nearby: App 2, #28-30

OBSCURE — POPULAR
OBSCUR-O-METER

MAP P. 34

Once upon a time there was a ramp. An elevated street ramp that crossed over the top of the Hoyt St. Rail Yards to connect Lovejoy St. to the Broadway Bridge. The Lovejoy Ramp. Under this Lovejoy Ramp worked a man. The man's work was holding up a stop sign to regulate car and train traffic. The intermittent work left time for the man to pursue his true passion— art. The man, in his earlier life, had been an accomplished artist, but now he was just a railroad worker with a sign in one hand… and a paintbrush in the other. In 1948, Tom Stefopolous began painting on the cement columns supporting the Lovejoy Ramp.

Portland City Archives

His lavish paintings drew immediate attention and praise. The legend of the Lovejoy Columns was born. Fifty years later, Tom had long since passed but much of his iconic art still remained under the soon-to-be-demolished Lovejoy Ramp. The ramp was slated for demolition as the decrepit Hoyt Rail Yards continued their evolution into today's Pearl District. The legend grew…and continues on to this day.

Of all the entries in this book the Lovejoy Columns are definitely a favorite oddity. "The Lovejoys," as we affectionately refer to the columns, are more than something to simply go and see. The Lovejoys are far more than just some age-old street art that were saved from destruction and put on public display—nope, the Lovejoys are the very fabric that adorns the Portland we love. The Lovejoys are more than just art, they are a story, but more than a story…a saga, a folklore…one of the weird Portland things that the phrase would have us "Keep." In essence the Lovejoys are everything this guidebook is about—something to see, something to learn, something to remember and lament and celebrate all at once.

In a nutshell, we feel that a short paragraph attempting to summarize the saga of the Lovejoys just doesn't cut it with us. We love the entire saga FAR TOO MUCH to give it short-shrift. If you go see the two columns that are now on display at the Elizabeth Lofts, on the columns themselves is a brief summary of the history that should satisfy someone with only mild curiosity. For the truly curious we take the timeline presented here and flesh it out on our website with the newspaper articles, photos, movie screengrabs, and links to Renwick's video in order to try to tell "the whole story." In addition we also include a treasure trove of Tom Stefopolous' art (which pre-dated the columns) that only came to public attention in 2013 thanks to the efforts of the Hellenic-American Cultural Center in Portland.

LOVEJOY'S TIMELINE

1927: Lovejoy Ramp built over Hoyt Rail Yards.

1948-52: Tom Stefopolous paints columns. Soon after both *Oregon Journal* and *Oregonian* run articles about the new paintings and the artist/ watchman behind them.

2 A   *Oregon Journal* SUNDAY, APRIL 25, 1948

AN "ARTIST-PENMAN,"–Tom E. Stefopoulos, 53, SP&S watchman at the NW 12th avenue and Lovejoy street crossing under the Broadway bridge ramp, has embellished the drab concrete supports with his de luxe doodling. Stefopoulos, Athens-born artist, studied seven years at the Greek National Art Institute before coming here in 1912. Once a commercial artist, he now has a temporary job as a watchman.

Oregon Journal 4-25-1948

10 *** THE SUNDAY OREGONIAN, AUGUST 22, 1948

Concrete Pillars of Lovejoy Ramp Provide Canvases For Mammoth Greek Drawings of Track Watchman

Art blooms in strange places but in all Portland perhaps the strangest is under the Lovejoy ramp to the Broadway bridge, where supports are gaudy with paintings by Greek-born Tom E. Stefopoulos, S. P. & S. track watchman, shown at work on a curly-tailed dove. Many of the paintings are religious, others stylized flower, foliage and animal motifs. A onetime penmanship champion and commercial artist, Stefopoulos says he now paints "just to kill time." (Photography by Frank Sterrett)

Oregonian 8-22-1948

continued ➡

1967: *Oregonian* runs an in-depth multi-page interview with Tom Stefopolous showing for the first time some of Tom's previous artwork.

Marvels of precision, control

Penwork by Tom Stefopoulos

Oregonian 3-12-1967

1970s-80s: Rail yards are largely abandoned, becoming a sort-of Portland "underground."

1989: Gus Van Sant uses the Lovejoy Columns as the backdrop for the intro and credits for *Drugstore Cowboy* (F4). The Lovejoys later appear in the Elliot Smith video *Lucky Three* (1996), and the Hollywood film *Foxfire* (1996) (F12).

1997-'99: Architectural group RIGGA and citizen group "Friends of the Columns" fight to save the columns from destruction once the Lovejoy Ramp becomes slated for demolition.

1999: (Sept.) Ramp is demolished but 10 columns are saved and "put to sleep" in an empty lot under the Fremont Bridge to await the funding and a place to re-erect them.

Oregonian 1-24-1999

Perils of the pillars

Portland's most treasured murals are saved — or are they? Tune in tomorrow

Lovejoy Graveyard

2000-2005: Funding to re-erect the columns never comes to fruition. Hopes are dashed, all looks bleak. The "protected" columns lay at rest but the protective coverings over the paintings suffer from weathering and vandalism.

2005: Vanessa Renwick displays her film-in-the-works "Lovejoy" in a Pearl District art-window display. Pearl developer John Carroll sees the video in the window and decides he can help with the plight of the columns.

2005-2006: John Carroll funds efforts to survey and conserve what is left of the columns' art while choosing the two best painted columns to erect in a plaza in front of his Elizabeth Lofts building. Hooray, Diogenes walks the streets of the Pearl again!

Elizabeth Lofts

2013-15: The Hellenic-American Cultural Center of Portland, avid supporter/promoters of all things Greek, organize the first-ever public showing of Tom Stefopolous' pre-columns artwork and fine penmanship. Eye-popping never-seen-before works of art, fully re-establishing Stefopolous as a respected artist rather than simply a watchman/graffiti-ist.

45

LOUIE, LOUIE

Where: 417 SW 13th, in the doorway of Solestruck shoes at Burnside

Google Coords ▶ 45.522612 -122.684293

Nearby: App 2, #26

MAP P. 34

OBSCURE — POPULAR

OBSCUR-O-METER

*Duh Duh Duh, duh duh...Me Gotta Go Now...*to see the new plaque mounted on the building where the Kingsmen recorded their legendary 1963 version of *Louie, Louie*. Not only did a commemorative plaque get re-mounted for the 50th Anniversary of the song's recording (a 30-year plaque had been made and mounted in 1993, but it was quickly stolen off the side of the building leaving just a glue smudge and four bolt-holes for 18 years)...not only that... but Mayor Charlie Hales was on hand to declare 10/5/2013 Portland's official "*Louie, Louie* Day."

NO WAY!

f*@k!

Pull up *Louie Louie* on YouTube and listen for second 55/56

Nowadays, there's nothing much LL-esque to see at the location of the former 2nd floor "Northwestern Inc. Recording Studio" because of 50 years of remodels. But it's neat to check out the plaque while you bring the Kingsmen up on your smartphone to rock-out where the world-famous *Louie, Louie* recording was made. *Duh Duh Duh, duh duh...OK, let's give it to 'em, **Right Now!***

Fun Louie, Louie oddities and eccentricities:

- Richard Berry wrote and recorded the original version of LL in 1956. It was a sort of Sea Chanty/Calypso tune. (YouTube)
- Berry copied the *"Duh Duh Duh, duh duh"* riff from an instrumental Cha-cha tune by Rene Touzet called *"El Loco Cha Cha"* (YouTube)

- A Seattle/Tacoma band, Rockin' Robin Roberts and the Wailers rescued the song from rock 'n' roll oblivion, recording it in 1961 with a zealous (and now famous) scream "Let's give it to them RIGHT NOW."
- The Kingsmen were a semi-popular Portland high school band circa 1960-63. They often, <u>very often</u>, covered the Rockin' Roberts version of LL because it made <u>everyone</u> dance. Playing live they sang the song with understandable/correct lyrics just like Rockin' Roberts' version.
- In April 1963 the Kingsmen headed to Northwestern Inc. Studio to record LL, the night after doing a live 90-minute marathon version of LL at Milwaukie's Chase Club. According to Dave Marsh's *Louie, Louie* book, Jack Ely's vocal cords were a little "shot" after the *Louie, Louie* marathon, the studio mic was hung too high and the band didn't know that their first take would be the only take they'd ever get a chance to record. <u>They were just warming up</u>, not trying to sing/play their best-ever LL.

- **<u>Funnest Fact:</u> At second 55-56 drummer Lynn Easton whacks his drumsticks wrong and squawks "fuck." Listen close, then wow your friends with this nearly-unknown nugget!**
- Original singer Jack Ely left the band before LL became a delayed smash hit. Drummer Lynn Easton becomes vocalist, as seen on 1965 Shindig Show. (YouTube)
- In 1964-65 the US Post office and the FBI "investigate" The Kingsmen's recording after numerous complaints that the lyrics were obscene. The FBI eventually concluded that the Kingsmen's lyrics were unintelligible at any speed and therefore not obscene.
- An estimated 1,600 cover versions have been recorded, making LL the most-all-time recorded rock song. EVER!
- Great LL versions to YouTube: Otis Redding, Black Flag, Toots & the Maytals, Iggy Pop, Fat Boys.

Duh Duh Duh, duh duh. Me gotta go now.

CURIOUSER? If you too get bit by the *Louie, Louie* Bug...start with Wikipedia, then proceed to Eric Predoehl's exhaustive LouieLouie.net, then, for graduate studies, read Dave Marsh's excellent tour-de-force *Louie, Louie Book.*

ANGLES ON BURNSIDE

Where: West Burnside Street

Google Coords 45.522856 -122.683856

Nearby: App 2, #26

OBSCUR-O-METER

Ever wonder why all the streets to the south of Burnside split off at an odd angle while the streets on the north side of Burnside form nice square intersections?

The reason dates back to Portland's earliest days, in 1845, just after Pettygrove and Lovejoy flipped their 1835 penny to decide on Portland as the name of their townsite. After Pettygrove won the flip (A12), the men then hired a surveyor to plat a grid of 16 waterfront blocks. These original platted blocks are still the same, basically 1st and 2nd streets between the Morrison and Hawthorne bridges (Washington St. to Jefferson St.). Surveyor Brown chose to align his two N-S streets roughly parallel to the bank of the Willamette, which happened to align almost perfectly with Magnetic North.

Portland City Archives photo

Thus, he aligned the first streets of Portland to Magnetic North and eventually all the streets in the original Lovejoy/Pettygrove plot were aligned the same way...up to the border at Burnside St. with "Couch's Addition."

Capt. Couch was the locally revered steamship captain who took a land claim for the square mile north of the Lovejoy claim, northwards of present-day Ankeny/Burnside Streets. Capt. Couch, according to Portland historian Eugene Snyder, being a seafaring man platted his addition to Portland, not to the compass-point north, but rather to True North. Snyder opines that Couch may have platted this 1866 addition towards True North because the Willamette Baseline had been surveyed in 1851, thus making all True North parceling much easier (Entry C6). The consequences of all this is that the streets meet on West Burnside at roughly a 21° angle because that was the declination difference between Magnetic North and True North in 1845.

This 21° angle has led to some interesting "wedge" buildings along Burnside between 10th and 20th streets. Sizzle Pie, at 10th, is actually shaped like a slice of pizza, as is the 1911 Buckingham Hotel Bldg. at 20th, which houses the Kingston Bar as well as another pizzeria, "Eat Pizza". The McMenamin's Ringlers Annex, at 13th, is housed in the 1917 Flatiron Bldg. which not only is shaped like an antique flatiron, but also mimics in miniature NYC's famous 1902 Flatiron skyscraper.

Portland Building's Mini Wooden City

Portland's Flatiron Bldg. (Ringlers)

New York's Flatiron Bldg.

CURIOUSER? How much of a map geek are you? If you hold a compass south of Burnside today you'll see that Magnetic North doesn't actually match-up with the direction of the streets. This is because the Magnetic North pole moves around over time and is nowadays less than 16° away from True North. BUT, if you enter the 1845 coordinates for Mag North into the GoogleEarth search box (69.09 -96.571), drop a pin there and then stretch a ruler path southwards until it hovers over PDX....Voilá, the 1845 Mag North direction matches the street angles perfectly. For non-super map geeks, Aimee has been so kind as to do this on a GoogleMaps overlay on our website.

POWELL'S BOOKS

Where: 1005 W. Burnside

Google Coords 45.523058 -122.681279

Nearby: App 4, #4

OBSCUR-O-METER
OBSCURE — POPULAR

Pre-Powell's, circa 1960s

What can we say about Powell's except…WE LOVE YOU! Biggest independent bookstore on the planet and one of the first bookstores in the country to put both new and used books together on the shelves—a move the naysayers doubted would be a success.

For the most part Powell's is a no-frills behemoth. They want to let the books speak for themselves—the attraction at Powell's is the books, not a fancy presentation. There are a couple of interesting oddities though. First, the Powell's building housed a car dealership before Michael Powell moved-in in 1979 and created the City of Books. Second, at the back entrance is a pillar carved out of sandstone in the likeness of a stack of books. The books are eight of the world's great books, each of their names carved in the language the book was originally printed in. *The Whale* was Moby Dick when the great white whale was still but a guppy (check Powells.com for *The Whale*'s tale). The Pillar of Books is also inscribed with four Latin phrases that sum-up Powell's business—go ahead, carpe diem while you carpe librum! And lastly, the ashes of a diehard Powell's fan are interred within the column—a true book lover's idea of heaven.

This is a special note from Scott, the co-author. I want to give Powell's a special shout-out because, personally, selling my self-published guidebooks to Powell's has been the highlight of my 12-year guidebook career. Also I want to express a special thank you to Brian Doerter, the long-time Powell's employee who got my first guidebook, *Curious Gorge*, into Powell's and has since encouraged and supported all my authoring forays. Thanks Brian and Gloria!

In my mind the pinnacle of my guidebook career, at least thus far, was in August 2010 when the just-released 3rd edition of *Curious Gorge* made it to as high as #3 on Powell's front-of-store Bestsellers shelf. That #3 spot is my proudest authoring achievement to date. Yes I like selling lots of books every year... yes I like getting fabulous reviews on Amazon...but what I'm most proud of is seeing one of my books on Powell's bestseller shelf every summer, all summer for the past five years. I'll never forget the excitement I felt in 2010 as *Curious Gorge* moved up the ranks and I wondered if it could possibly get to #1! It never did move up further, but it did hang in the top-ten all summer and fall. I had tasted Powell's glory and I felt really proud that I had finally crafted a guidebook that people were passionate about.

So, to be honest, my personal goal for PDXccentric is to get to #1 at Powell's. I hope we've written a great guidebook and I hope Portlanders will love it...but, as they say, the proof will be in the Powell's. Sure I hope to sell heaps of books all over the city at the myriad of local shops we'll stock, but truth-be-told, nothing would make me prouder than getting to #1 at the World's Best Bookstore!

Check Facebook and our website for photo-updates on whether we've made it onto the bestseller shelf…and how high we've managed to creep. Thanks for buying our book, cheers,

Photo by Brian Doerter

POD (SHORT PEOPLE GOT NO REASON TO...)

Where: 10th and West Burnside

 45.522880 -122.681335

Nearby: App 4, #4

MAP P. 34

OBSCURE · POPULAR
OBSCUR-O-METER

Pod, locally known as Satan's Testicle, is the quizzical kinetic sculpture located across the street from Powells' Burnside entrance. *Pod* is undoubtedly PDX's most fun interactive sculpture...for some. This playful swinging bulb, intended by the artist to somehow represent Portland's "infrastructure, energy and vibrancy" swings wildly to-and-fro on its double gimbals...only if you're tall enough to reach the hanging ball.

Is it possible that *Pod* designer Pat Beeman was a bit of a closet Randy Newman fan? Because, as Pod stands on its three legs, anyone who's shorter than 5'6" "ain't got no reason to" try (as Randy Newman sang in his infamous hit song *Short People*).

Regardless of your personal vertical challenges, step up and give *Pod* a try, we're sure you'll have a ball...but just know, at *Pod*, size does matter.

5' 5"

5' 7"

6' 2"

CURIOUSER? Google: "Voodoo Doughnut's Tres Shannon Reviews Storm Large in Los Angeles," whence Tres comments on Storm singing the songs of Randy (while accompanied by stars from both *Spinal Tap* and *Married with Children*.) Odd.

ALIS VOLAT PROPRIIS

Where: 401 SW 5th Ave.

Google Coords ▶ 45.520622 -122.676697

Nearby: Entry A1; App 2, #5-6; App 4, #4-5; Entry C9

OBSCUR-O-METER

"Alis Volat Propriis" is Oregon's official state motto…yet it remains a sort of motto non gratis, a motto rarely known, rarely spoken, rarely seen. That is, except, amongst a legion of Oregon women who are so enraptured with our state motto that they tattoo it all over their lithesome bodies. *Alis Volat Propriis*, or, "She Flies with Her Own Wings" flocks to the feminine nooks and crannies like Swifts flock to a chimney. Look behind the neck, under

the boob, down the side, between the blades, above the crack, atop the foot… or in the case of renowned Blink-182 porn starlet Janine Lindemulder…well let's just say her kitty "purrs with her own wings."

Alis Volat Propriis is probably the most-celebrated state motto in America, but strangely, it's probably the least-known motto, even in Oregon. **Here's why:** this catchy Latin phrase was chosen in the 1840s as the motto of the still-in-infancy Oregon Territory. But, as the independently-minded territory moved towards statehood in the late 1850s the powers-that-be decided to coin a newer and more politicized motto that would reflect our territory's affiliation with the Union's side in the contentious slavery/Civil War debate. Thus, *"The Union"* became Oregon's motto, soon emblazoned on both the state seal and flag as Oregon became the 33rd state. Like the failed wings of Icarus, Oregon's original motto crashed and burned, replaced by the dullest of all state mottos. Hail *The Union*….oh, ho-hum.

Fast forward a century to 1957 and the Oregon legislature finally got around to formalizing *The Union* as the "official" state motto, even though the motto recognized a barely-remembered political affiliation. So…how come *The Union* is still on our state seal and flag, given *Alis Volat Propriis* is nowadays our official state motto? Seems that in 1987 an influential and wise state historian, Cecil Edwards, teamed up with State Senator Barbara Roberts (and others) to champion a bill to re-motto Oregon to its former-motto'd glory. Like a phoenix, *A.V.P.* rose from the cold ashes of history to flap her wings once again…but where to did she fly? She didn't fly her way back onto either the flag or state seal…nor most anywhere

Territory seal on Bank Bldg at 5th & Stark

else visible except maybe the delicate skin of some PDX-chromosomers. Seems the 1987 bill changed the official motto while leaving the flag and the state seal as-was. Humph.

Around PDX the only outdoor place you'll see the *A.V.P.* phrase is adorning a frieze above the ornate entrance of the former First National Bank of Portland (most recently Bank of the West) at SW 5th and Stark. Why *A.V.P.* and the territorial seal are emblazed on this 1916 building is anyone's guess.

For Xccentric xtra credit, it turns out that Googling state mottos is kinda fun. Do citizens of other states also tattoo their mottos all over themselves? Check out Michigan's lame one, *Si Quaeris Peninsulam Amoenam Circumspice*—hahahaha, no tatts for that one! What about the sexist Maryland motto *Fatti maschii, parole femine*, which translates to "Manly Deeds, Womanly Words"—which hipster would brave that one on their skin? Kansas has a catchy Latin phrase with a neat story behind it, and, strangely, GoogleImage reveals a trove of *Aspera/Astra* tattoos, but the phrasing of the words seems to need to be reversed to make the motto under-the-boob worthy. North Carolina's *Esse Quam Videri*, "To Be, Rather than to Seem" also gets some ink of approval, though not as picturesque a fashion as Oregon's. Seems like Oregon and our 1987 re-born motto now wins the State-motto-as-art derby. Thanks Cecil, thanks Barbara!

Janine's tattoo

CURIOUSER? There is a call out to our state motto in the Oregon State Building at 800 NE Oregon Street in the form of a brass ring hanging from the ceiling in the lobby engraved with *Alis Volat Propriis* on one side and *She Flies With Her Own Wings* on the other. Above it, on the second floor, a bird hangs from the ceiling.

THE CAR WASH FOUNTAIN

Where: SW 5th & Ankeny

Google Coords ▶ 45.522708 -122.675289

Nearby: App 1, #4; App 4, #4-5

B10

MAP P. 34

OBSCURE   POPULAR

OBSCUR-O-METER

The Car Wash Fountain is an enigma.

1st off, though fancy and expensive to build and operate, it got emplaced in 1977 without being named. Huh? The peeps of PDX would have none of that nouveau-mindedness and quickly nicknamed it "Car Wash" for its tendency to spritz passing cars when the wind kicked up. C'mon though…how can you have an unnamed public space? What would you say to a friend? "Wanna meet me at the unnamed fountain off Burnside near the 24-hour Church of Elvis so we can trade Elliott Smith cassettes?" What if this imaginary friend thought you meant the dribbly Lee Kelly Fountain on the west side of Big Pink. Shit, that friend would be pissed, and no *Roman Candle* for you.

2nd off, the Car Wash Fountain is an enigma because it's mostly <u>OFF</u>. 'Twasn't always so, this OFF-ness. For six years the Car Wash rocked-out just like that 1976 Rose Royce one-hit wonder. But alas, with the 1983 erection of Big Pink (US BanCorp Tower)…the Car Wash fell on hard times. Seems that the erection of Big Pink caused a new urban wind-tunnel which blew the Car Wash's mists over towards the entrance of the BanCorp Tower, annoying the hoi-polloi who worked in the pink skyscraper. Oh my, in an edifice as innuendo-prone as Big Pink you surely wouldn't want to encourage workplace impropriety by showing up for work with wet spots on your trousers, stains on your blue dress, or, gasp, a moistened silk blouse. Big Pink had an insur-erection on its hands—nobody wanted a blow before their job! To quell the snickering and stop the spritzing the Car Wash's on/off button was shackled to an anemometer in the hope that this would stop the Car Wash from blowing Big Pink. Check it out—atop the light pole next to the Car Wash you'll see the 3-cup spinning wind gauge. Supposedly, according to the city's fountain engineer, when the wind blows more than "5-8 mph" the fountain shuts itself off, allowing the Pink peeps to enter their building without pink faces. After 60 seconds

of no blowing the fountain is supposed to turn itself back on. Trouble is, the system hasn't worked properly for the past few years, even with an anemometer upgrade. Sometimes Big Pink still gets blown.

Nowadays, the Car Wash is an Xccentric favorite because every time we walk/drive/bike on Burnside we always first look to see if the trees are blowing and then make a bet whether or not the Car Wash will be on. To the unknown wind-tunnel effect you have to add-in whether you think the Parks Bureau will have the thing fixed properly. Tough statistical modeling to keep our retired citizens sharp.

VOODOO DOUGHNUT

Where: 22 SW 3rd Ave.

Google Coords ▶ 45.522576 -122.673157

Nearby: App 1, #4; App 4, #4-5

OBSCURE · POPULAR
OBSCUR-O-METER

MAP P. 34

When the phrase "Keep Portland Weird" was hijacked from Austin, Texas in 2003, the newly opened Voodoo Doughnut was just starting to define weirdness. Originally, the closet-sized shop was only open from late night to early morning. Weird. Sell doughnuts, cash only, at weird hours to weird oft-drunk night crawlers. Ain't no Krispy Kreme here yo. Weirder yet was the eccentric doughnuts that sprang from the creative minds of founders Cat Daddy Pogson and Tres Shannon. Nyquil, Pepto Bismol, Tums, Tang, Fruit Loops…Cock 'n' Balls…um, yup, not your father's do-nuts these….Voodoos are Portland's dough-nuts.

What's weird to us authors is how captivating the story of Voodoo, and especially Tres Shannon, has become to us. Truth-be-told, a couple of years ago neither Aimee nor I gave a flip about Tres, Cat Daddy and Voodoo. But then, like so much in this book, we began digging deeper into the story behind Voodoo and we became entranced, as if Baron Semedi had cast a spell. In a nutshell, we've come basically full-circle and now see Tres Shannon as a sort of quintessential poster boy for the concept of Portland being weird, eccentric, quirky, odd…or whatever label you want. We say this with the highest esteem—Tres was "weird" way before weird became cool, before "weird" became Portland's calling card. In many ways Tres himself has shepherded-in the weird.

Don't take our word for it though. We're just guidebook chroniclers. And since this is a guidebook and not a biography, we simply want to give you some hints as to where to look to learn about Tres Shannon, the birth of "weird" Portland, and the story behind Voodoo's success.

Tres Shannon runs for Mayor
Oregonian 4/28/1992

1. **Watch the DVD _X-Ray Visions_** about the all-ages music/performance club X-Ray Café that Tres and Ben Ellis ran from 1990-94, just around the corner from Voodoo on Burnside. This is a brilliant, chaotic chronicle of "pre-weird" early-'90s Portland that seems far far weirder than today's Portland. Many people credit the X-Ray as the birthplace of "weird." Amongst all the chaotic oddness, you'll also get to see Richard Elliott Shannon III (Tres) campaign for mayor in 1992 (_Oregonian_ articles on our website). Strangely, Voodoo

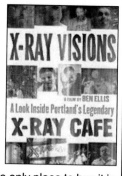

doesn't sell this little-known hour-long DVD. The only place to buy it in town is at Microcosm Publishing up on N. Williams.

2.
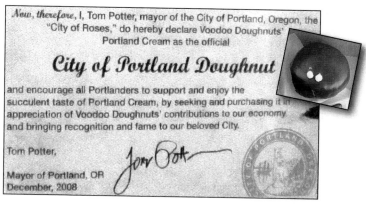

Tres has been the front man/MC for nearly 22 years for this world-famous live-band karaoke performance. They play Monday nights at Dante's (across street from Voodoo). Tres is showman supreme, while Dawn and the rest of the revolving band members are super tight. **Karaoke from Hell is MUST-SEE Portland good weirdness!** If you are a first-time PDX visitor, seeing/singing with KFH is arguably the quintessential "weird" Portland experience. Go see—the cast of characters who regularly sing are outrageous!

3. **Voodoo created what is now Portland's "official" doughnut**, the Portland Cream Doughnut, so-sanctioned by Mayor Tom Potter as his last action as mayor in 2008. In a master-stroke of pure eccentric genius, Tres and Cat Daddy added two white dots (eyes) to a typical cream-filled doughnut (a-la Boston), adding the eyes because, "Portland has vision." Of course unlike the Boston version of the doughnut that lacks vision. Fucking brilliant! Bravo. PDXccentric's favorite doughnut by far!

continued ➡

Voodoo Bites

If you are waiting in line outside of Voodoo Old town...

Three "weird" neighborhood things to Google on your smartphone to enhance your line time:

1. The "Keep Portland Weird" mural on the back of Dante's. Portland shanghai'd the motto from Austin, Texas. Check Wikipedia.

2. The Paris Theater. The hard-to-read decrepit marquee to the north of Voodoo. Who knew that this adult theater once played *Deep Throat* for five straight years? www.RaysParisTheater.com

3. Embassy Suites Hotel, kitty-corner from Voodoo. This grand hotel opened as the Multnomah Hotel in 1912, and as a publicity stunt allowed a young pilot named Silas Christofferson to take-off and fly off the roof in a primitive biplane over a crowd of 50,000 Rose Parade gawkers. What a stunt! Google Silas Christofferson (Inside the hotel lobby is an airplane model w/pix). *Portland Mercury*'s 6/11/2012 online article has historic photos and a video link to a firsthand account of the flight.

Videos to watch:

1. American Hipster #38: Voodoo Doughnut
2. Anthony Bourdain's "No Reservations" visits Voodoo with Chuck Palahniuk
3. GimmeDoughnut.com

Things to look for as you near the Voodoo order counter:

1. Above the entrance, along with stained-glass renditions of both Cat Daddy and Tres, you'll see a trio of the most-famed Voodoos. Portland Cream, Maple Bacon, and Voodoo. Get some—these three will REALLY put the magic in your box.

2. Voodoo remodeled in 2011, taking over the old corner entrance of the transitioning Berbati's Pan music venue (where Tres had booked the bands for the previous decade). At the new Voodoo door you can still see PAN tiled-into the entrance floor, as well as a horny-headed Pan visage adorning the pillar. Also, as a tribute to late Berbati's owner Ted Papaioannou, his face graces the stained glass panel furthest down the alley.

3. Inside, on the far wall, is the Isaac Hayes black velvet painting. This is one of Tres' fondest treasures from his old X-Ray Café. After the X-Ray closed in 1994, the Isaac travelled the country in Cat Daddy's possession. Upon opening Voodoo in May 2003 the painting came home to become Voodoo's "soul channeler." Each of the four Voodoo locations now has its own velvet soul.

BENJAMIN BRINK/THE OREGONIAN

Tres Shannon (left), co-owner of Downtown Portland's Voodoo Doughnut, and doughnut chef Jay Rubin describe how their giant plastic-foam wall doughnut was damaged during an attempted pre-midnight heist Monday.

Oregonian 1-19-2005

4. Inside on the ceiling is the original large Styrofoam doughnut that had nearly been stolen out of the original Voodoo in 2005. This fabulous attempted-theft of Voodoo's most-holey icon made headlines in the *Oregonian* in Jan. 2005. The story is a classic. In short, as thief Neiderbach tried to hustle the massive doughnut out the door other customers fought with him until he fled. Tres was called in off the stage over at Dante's where he had been Karaoke-From-Hell'ing. Mayhem ensued…Neiderbach in cuffs…Voodoo later creating a vile doughnut in Neiderbach's dis-honor. Shortly after some Voodoo fans penned a song to commemorate the debacle—"The Ballad of Fryer Jay". This little-known ditty can be heard on the little-known Voodoo-doco *Gimme Doughnut* (details of the theft, headlines, and video link are on our website).

CURIOUSER? Ever wonder where Cat Daddy got his name? Turns out "Cat Daddy" is a nickname for a charming man-about-town in the South where Kenneth Pogson has his roots. It was the name he used as a local Professional Wrestling announcer.

SIGN HUNG WRONG?

Where: Corner of NW 3rd & Couch

Google Coords ▶ **45.523901 -122.673301**

Nearby: App 1, #4; App 2, #27; App 4, #4-5

MAP P. 34

OBSCURE · POPULAR
OBSCUR-O-METER

The sorta-famous Hung Far Low sign hung outside the 2nd-floor Hung Far Low restaurant/cocktail lounge for 80 years, from 1928-2008. This is just a block north of the ornate Chinatown gate on 5th and Burnside. The original Hung Far Low was a classic Chinatown dive, serving super-stiff cocktails and semi-gooey chop suey. This was back when Chinatown was a part of the run-down pre-2000s Old Town District.

As Old Town began renovating, circa 2005 (largely due to the efforts of civic-hero Bill Naito), the Hung Far Low restaurant moved out of the increasing upscaling to relocate on the east side's gritty 82nd Ave. After Hung Far Low moved, the classic sign stayed put until the restaurant Ping began renovations of the building. But hey, instead of replacing the classic sign with a new Ping sign, the business, the city, and the PDX people cried-out to save the Hung Far Low sign. Yup, even though the business had moved across town and the sign was totally dilapidated and required removal, the Portland Development Commission and concerned citizens cadged-together $77k in the midst of the 2009 "great recession" in order to re-make and re-erect a sign for a no-longer-there business.

Does this make sense, or is it just more Quirky Portland? Noted "Portland Architecture" critic/blogger Brian Libby opined in a 2010 post, *"When is a decayed building sign from a long-gone Chinese Restaurant more than that...what inspires people to spend $77,000 in a terrible recession to re-erect an obsolete chop suey sign?"* Hmmm? By the end of his post, though, Libby comes around to supporting the re-erection of Hung Far Low.

Portland City Archives 1969

What do you think? Is it odd to re-erect a historic sign for a business that still exists elsewhere in the city? Is this a sign hung wrong?

RE-ERECT THE HUNG FAR LOW SIGN **BENEFIT SHOW**

WITH YOUR HOST TRES SHANNON OF VOODOO DONUTS!

CHOP SUEY HUNG FAR LOW COCKTAILS

DIAMOND TUCK
PINEHURST KIDS
BOO FROG FEAT. CHRIS NEWMAN
NETHER REGIONS - THE ROSENBALMS
RECORDS BY ROCK THROWER
PLUS AN ASSAULT BY THE LAST REGIMENT OF SYNCOPATED DRUMMERS!!

SATYRICON - FRI SEPT 11 - 8PM

CURIOUSER? Watch the great PDX Development Commission video on YouTube (link on our website). Also we have *Oregonian* ads from the 1928 opening. The awning of the still in Old Town Hung Far Low is visible in a quick scene in *Down & Out with the Dolls* (F14).

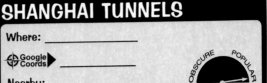

SHANGHAI TUNNELS

Where: _____

Google Coords ▶ _____

Nearby: _____

OBSCUR-O-METER

The existence of Shanghai Tunnels is Portland's most popular urban myth. Throughout the research/writing of this book, whenever Aimee or I explained to people we were writing about Portland's oddities, the comment almost always came back, "Oh, like the Shanghai Tunnels." Popular myth, but not true. Yes, there were once waterfront tunnels, and yes, 1800s sailors were "crimped" for indentured labor on ocean going ships…but nope, there's no evidence that the tunnels played any part in the crimping. Yes, there are a number of tours that play up this myth, but also a number of tours that debunk the myth.

The Last Word on Shanghai Tunnels - Including 14 reasons why the stories are bogus
—Author Barney Blalock

Here at PDXccentric we feel no need to laboriously attack the myth because we have keen local historians who have already shredded it.

READ AND LEARN, LISTEN AND LEARN... THEN SPEAK OF THIS SHANGHAI MYTH NO MORE.

Finn JD John.
His excellent book *Wicked Portland* as well as on his website *Offbeat Oregon History* gives the myth a solid debunk.

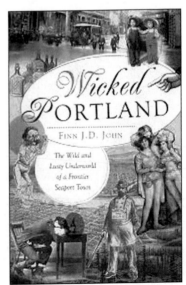

Doug Kenck-Crispin.

The Mastermind behind online *Kick-Ass Oregon History* at www.ORHistory.com takes the myth to task on a well researched 2-part podcast.

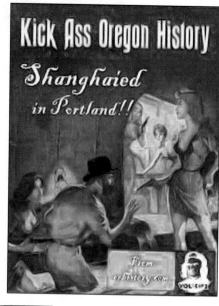

Barney Blalock.

Barney's book *Portland's Lost Waterfront* firmly nails shut the coffin over the myth. Online you can read his definitive 14-point debunking on his Portland Waterfront History Blog.

CURIOUSER? Online *Willamette Week* review of "Portland's Lost Waterfront." Watch OPB video *Oregon Experience*: "Portland Noir." Links on our website.

B
1
4

MAGNET AND STEEL

Where: Old Town, either side of Burnside

⊕ Google Coords ▶ **45.523834 -122.670845**

Nearby: App 1, #4; App 2, #27

MAP P. 34

OBSCUR-O-METER

Downtown-North

Like the nearly-forgotten 1978 soft-rock hit *Magnet and Steel*, Portland also had a huge '70s hit with its downtown-core heavy metal. But Portland's metal years where a century before Walter Egan's and Portland's 1870s metal never rocked—it clad.

The magnetic side of the Blagen Bldg.

Portland is home to the 2nd largest collection of still-standing cast-iron clad buildings in America, next only to NYC's Soho district. Architecture buffs work themselves into a tizzy when contemplating the fact that 90% of Portland's commercial downtown was built with cast-iron stylings from the 1850s to the 1880s. Sadly

66

though, only a portion of this magnetic architecture escaped both the fire of 1873 and the wrecking ball of the 1940s-60s. Still, Portland's Old Town has the best metal in all the West.

Truth-be-told, our opinion is that PDX's cast-iron architectural wonderland is only of mild interest to most normal folk who have an entire city chock full of Xccentricities to explore…except…except…**if you have a magnet in hand!** To us Xccentrics, fun is standing in front of an ornate façade, guessing whether it is actually cast-iron or a knock-off look-alike imposter…then reaching out with a magnet to "test the metal." Yup, call us weird perhaps, but have you ever tossed a magnet at a building to see if it sticks? No? Then we rest our case. PDXamining historic buildings

continued ➡

with a magnet in hand is <u>so</u> <u>damn</u> <u>fun</u> you might even let out a little ferrous squeal when a building surprises you. Strangely enough, some buildings look metal and aren't and, vice versa, some look aren't and are. Trust us. No wait, don't trust us—go see for yourself.

Knowing that few people carry a handy magnet in their pocket anymore, lest it erase their credit cards, we uber-rich self-published authors are gonna hide some magnets—those hyper-magnetic little discs—in a hidden-yet-convenient Old Town-esque location so that you can saunter by and take <u>one</u> of the magnets for a curious little walkabout. Better yet, bring your bike so you can pedal to the metal. C'mon now though, we implore you

Check the PDXccentric website for magnet location updates

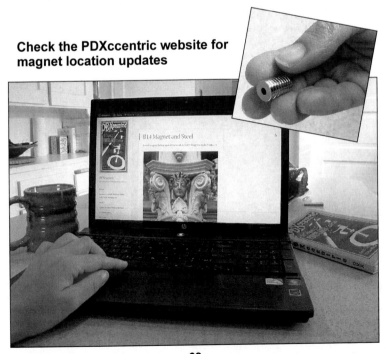

not to "steel" the li'l magnets or there'll be none for the next Xccentric to play with. How would you feel if you got to the hidden spot and no magnets were to be found? Please just take the magnet for a walk and then put it back—Google Street-view cameras will be watching you! Alas, we know the magnets will disappear…and some magnets might get tossed too high to reach…and…and, etc etc, yada, yada. Thus, Aimee pledges to check-up and restock the hiding spot every couple weeks to keep the fun ferrous flux flowing. We may remark, "Who the flux stole all the magnets?"…but we'll keep the restocking for at least a year. Promise.

We won't reveal the current hiding spot in print here though, because we figure we'll have to change now and again once the ne'er-do-wells suss it out. Thus, you'll have to check our website page for this entry to find the latest mini-mag hiding spot.

Five Favorite Facades

1. <u>Blagen Block:</u> NW 1st & Couch. The Blagen Block Building takes the cake. Not only are there faces galore—Lady Liberty, lions and bizarre bearded men—there are also what appears to be green-painted hops hanging above the archways. Holy IBU! And, with the magnet in hand be sure to check out the surprisingly non-magnetic north side of the block.

2. <u>Ankeny Square:</u> SW 1st & Ankeny. The square is decorated with bits of façade from Portland's torn-down architecture. Some historic plaques complement the scene surrounding the 1888 Skidmore fountain.

3. <u>New Market Building:</u> SW 2nd & Ash. The most ornate and extensive cast-iron façade in Portland. Check the west side for the roofline building date and look up to the SE corner roof to see an odd iron elk statue.

4. <u>Merchant Hotel:</u> NW 3rd & Davis. Home to Old Town Pizza and other bars. Big female faces (iron maidens) gaze down from the façade, and look for the Willamette Iron Works plaque on the north side. Head inside to visit the neat secluded "haunted" courtyard.

5. <u>Fecheimer & White Building:</u> SW Naito Parkway & Oak. This small building has OK metal and a Willamette Iron Works plaque, but more interesting and overlooked is the squat Hallock Building next door (to the south) which is surprisingly Portland's oldest commercial building, dating from 1857.

WHAT'S YOUR SIGN?

Where: West end of the Burnside Bridge

 45.523318 -122.670445

Nearby: Entry E3; App 1, #4;
App 2, #27; Entry C9

OBSCUR-O-METER

B15

MAP P. 34

Downtown-North

(Note: most tellings of the White Stag sign history have numerous errors, some minor, some major. We believe the timeline presented here to be the most accurate yet, sourced from Amalgamated, Ramsay, Oregonian Archives, and a myriad of internet half-truths.)

The White Stag sign is Portland's favorite landmark. Since 2010 the neon sign has touted "Portland Oregon," but for the previous 70 years the famed sign advertised a succession of three different Oregon-based businesses. Kind of weird that in a city as gorgeous as Portland, rife with bridges, statues, fountains, plazas,

etc...the most identifiable landmark was a neon business advertisement. Over and over for the past 40 years the citizens and politicians have rallied to the cause of keeping the White Stag sign erect and illuminated, especially the red nose of Rudolph which has added cheer to the holidays since 1958. In 1977 the sign officially became an ordained "Portland landmark," the first and only local advertisement so honored. Over the years the White Stag sign has been compared, in terms of civic identity, to none less than Seattle's Space Needle, San Francisco's Golden Gate, St. Louis' Arch and NYC's Smithsonian. High praise indeed, but you gotta wonder if 'Frisco thinks our sign is just as iconic as their bridge?

Regardless, this sign, in all its various incarnations, has been standing for roughly half of Portland's existence and it sure has seen some sights. Imagine witnessing from its lofty perch the construction of four new Willamette bridges, the removal of the Harbor Freeway, a flood that erased Vanport, a volcano that blew its top, a copper goddess on a barge...and countless other civic milestones. Long live our White Stag! *Rudolph with your nose so bright, won't you guide our sleigh tonight*...and for every other night yet to come.

Eras of the White Stag Sign

Big Sugar Sign 'Beets' All

Oregonian 3-3-40

Photo courtesy of Don Nelson

1940-1957

1938: The Amalgamated Sugar Co. of Utah opens its first Oregon factory in Nyssa to produce White Satin Sugar out of Oregon-grown sugar beets.

1940: The company commissions with Ramsay Signs to erect a billboard atop the White Stag building to advertise White Satin Sugar as "Oregon's Own and Only".

1951: Amalgamated Sugar changes the White Satin logo from the bullseye circle to a cursive font. In late 1951 Ramsay changes the White Satin sign to put the cursive font into the Oregon outline, thus beginning the angled-font era that the sign is now famous for (photos of this cursive era are <u>extremely</u> hard to find).

1952: Amalgamated opens a Portland distribution plant on Columbia Blvd. (which still exists today).

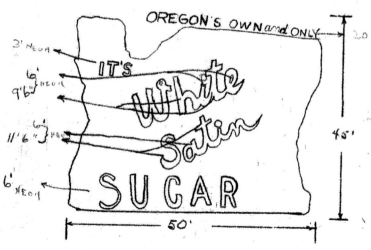

Drawing from sign-change permit 9-28-51

continued ➡

71

1956: A new ad campaign for White Satin begins and the company drops the billboard lease (exact details have been hard to ascertain).

Photo Courtesy of Amalgamated Sugar

1957-1997

1957: The White Stag Sportswear company begins leasing the billboard. They have Ramsay put "White Stag" in angled cursive, just as White Satin had been, and also include their trademark stag on the top of the Oregon outline (White Stag being a translation of the founders' names Weis and Hirsch). The company owns the building underneath the sign, it being their HQ where they produce their nationally-renowned sportswear.

1973: White Stag leaves the building for a new Portland HQ and sells the building to Bill Naito/ Norcrest China. White Stag continues to lease the sign.

1977: The "White Stag Sign" is designated an official Portland landmark, saving it from the "Beautify Portland" anti-billboard movement that marked the end of Portland's neon-crazed era.

1986: White Stag leaves Portland altogether (after 102 years) but keeps paying for sign.

1989: White Stag/Warnaco ceases paying for sign and the sign goes dark all summer. Bill Naito steps up and begins paying for the White Stag sign out of his own generous pocket in the name of civic spirit.

Oregonian 11-1-86

1996: Bill Naito passes away. The sign needs a major overhaul and remaining Naito family is unwilling to pay the large bill to advertise a company not their own. They begin negotiations with city's landmarks committee to advertise the Naito-owned stores "Made in Oregon."

1997-2010

1997: An agreement is reached between Naito/Portland/Ramsay to change sign from "White Stag" to "Made in Oregon" and replace "Sportswear" with "Old Town." A ten-year lease is signed and Rudolph's nose lights-up once again in time for Xmas season.

2006: University of Oregon leases the White Stag building from Naito Corp./(new owner) and takes over "Made in Oregon" sign payments.

2008: University of Oregon petitions landmark committee to change the sign to "University of Oregon." Controversy erupts. In 2009 anti "Univ. of Oregon" wording-change heats up, pitting Commissioner Randy Leonard (PSU grad) against the University president. Negotiations stall and tempers flare as Leonard threatens the University with an eminent domain sign takeover.

2009: University of Oregon steps away from embattled sign and doesn't renew the sign lease, leaving the "Made in Oregon" sign in limbo.

2010-Present

2010: A deal for new "Portland Oregon" sign takes shape. The building owner donates the rooftop space and $200,000 to update and changeover sign in exchange for parking and lease considerations. Ramsay donates sign to the city with the city now paying Ramsay $2000 per month for upkeep.

2010: In September the new "Portland Oregon" sign goes up and thus far, stays up.

CURIOUSER? The White Stag/Portland Oregon Sign has been featured in a handful of movies. A couple of our favorite cameos are: The movie *Ironheart* (F9) where you get to see the sign still reading White Stag and it is pictured both in day and lit up at night. The 1997 movie *Bongwater* where at minute 1:14 you see the sign in the process of being dismantled from its era of reading White Stag, in the scene only the W_ _te S_ _ _ remain. History caught on film. Also see *The Auteur* (F17) and *Down and Out With the Dolls* (F14) where the sign reads Made in Oregon.

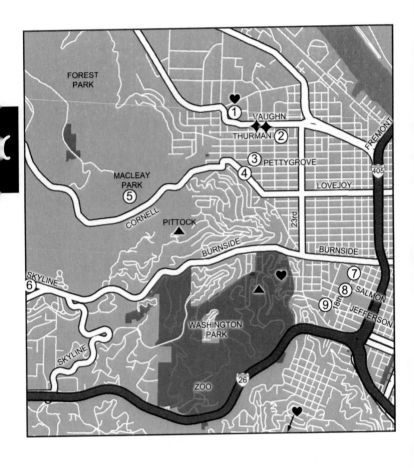

OUTER WEST PORTLAND

APPENDIX KEY

♥ Hot, Not, or Learn-a-lot Statues

✦ Custom Bike Racks

★ Intersection Murals

▲ Viewpoints

C 1

GUILDS LAKE, FORESTRY BUILDING, MONTGOMERY WARD

Where: NW 27th & Vaughn streets

Google Coords ▶ 45.537443 -122.708684

Nearby: App 1, #1; App 2, #31-32

MAP P. 74

OBSCURE   POPULAR
OBSCUR-O-METER

Outer West

Guilds Lake isn't there anymore, nor is the Forestry Building, nor Montgomery Ward. So why is there anything here to read? Well, you guessed right. We <u>can</u> find PDXccentricity in even the minutiae of local history and then weave an overly verbose and pun-addled entry. Here we go....

Guilds Lake was once an idyllic wetland-like lake occupying much of what's now the industrial Slabtown district. Guilds Lake had its heyday in 1905 when Portland hosted the Lewis and Clark Centennial Exposition. Around/in Guilds Lake was built a gorgeous, fancy, ornate "White City," patterned after Chicago's 1893 World's Fair (check Larson's novel *Devil*

Portland City Archives photo

76

in the White City). The Expo was Portland's very first "day in the sun," attracting gazillions of visitors and really putting Portland on the map. At the Expo, the one thing—a VERY BIG thing—that wasn't white was the Forestry Building, built of Simon Benson's logs. It was nicknamed the world's biggest log cabin...because it was. Photos of its construction and interior are Amazing! So, after a fabulous five-month run, the Expo closed on schedule and all the buildings were removed as per the land-lease agreement. Most of the buildings were simply torn down since they had been built as temporary structures. However, a few were removed and reassembled in new locations. The mammoth log cabin was the only building that remained on site.

Thus, in 1906 Guilds Lake went back to being a lake, but not for long. Onto the scene waltzed Lafayette (Lafe) Pence with many a scheme brewing in his devious mind. The first was to claim water rights on almost <u>all</u> Portland's streams, including Bull Run, in a sneaky attempt to make Portland buy its water from him, even though the city had already been utilizing Bull Run water for 10 years. This scheme was foiled. Next scheme was to buy Guilds Lake as well as the West Hills above it. Lafe's grand plan was to hydro-blast the hills, shaping them into buildable terraces, while sluicing the dirt removed from the hills down to Guilds Lake, thus filling in portions of the lake to create valuable new industrial acreage. A great visionary plan...except Lafe skipped on some details. Long story short, great plan but poor execution, costing Lafe a fortune and ushering him off the Portland scene. But his plan wasn't for naught and soon proper Portland bigwigs got together to better execute the same plan. Thus, the Westover Terraces were crafted out of the hills while Guilds Lake shrank as its shores became buildable acreage. (More on Westover at the end of this story.)

Portland grew substantially due to the success of the Lewis and Clark Exposition. Industry embraced the former-lake land and in 1920 Montgomery Ward built a huge warehouse/showroom directly beside the HUGE log cabin Forestry Building. Fast forwarding to 1964, most of Guilds Lake had been filled-in by Army Corps dredge from the Columbia River

channel. The aging log cabin still stood next to Montgomery Ward...until the log cabin caught fire and burned to the ground, a fire so hot and beyond control that it actually warped and bowed the window framing on the near corner of the Montgomery Ward building (amazingly, still visible today— SW corner).

1964 Fire

Portland Fire Department photo

continued ➡

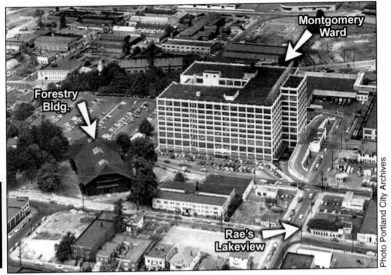

Montgomery Ward

Forestry Bldg.

Rae's Lakeview

By 1985 Montgomery Ward had been long-shuttered. PDX developer-hero Bill Naito bought the building and extensively refurbished the interior, leaving the outside with the age-old look we have today… except for the W and D from Ward being replaced by a P and K, thus creating a new name for this visual icon. Inside the impressive Montgomery Park building, up top in the vast atrium, you'll see a white Venus de Arles statue, reminiscent of the many Greek statues that decorated the 1905 Exposition. (Close-ups

Venus de Arles super zoom photo

78

reveal that Venus holds "The Apple of Discord," as well as a mirror. These are the same things Venus De Milo would be holding if she still had arms... but that's another story. See App 1, #1)

Places to Visit:

- SW corner of Montgomery Park to see the slight bowing.

- Across the street uphill from Montgomery Park is the "Forestry Commons" apartments built on the site of the burnt log cabin (Info plaques at the entrance detail the details).

- **Guilds Lake Inn.** On NW 29th off of Hwy 30. This 6am to 3pm diner features the best display of 1905 Exposition photos anywhere (not to mention a pretty damn good sandwich). Check out the exquisite above-counter Portland panorama from 1903.

- **Rae's Lakeview Lounge.** This restaurant/bar takes its name from the lake that it doesn't overlook. We like that...and we like cold beer...and we like the Drugstore Cowboy menu cover w/Lovejoys. Also, lots of 1905 pix inside.

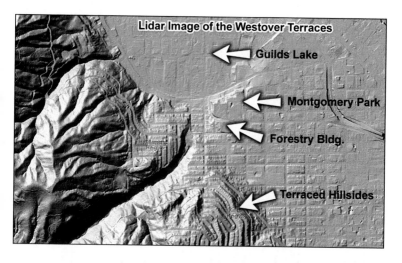

Lidar Image of the Westover Terraces
Guilds Lake
Montgomery Park
Forestry Bldg.
Terraced Hillsides

CURIOUSER? Check out the DOGAMI Lidar website. This is the extra bit about Westover Terraces. In person (or via Google Earth), this hillside development looks like, well, an unremarkable hillside development. But, geek-out and zoom in on the Lidar view and Whoa, the century-old terracing pops out, contrasting the developed hillsides of say, Council Crest.
Check: http://www.oregongeology.org/dogamilidarviewer, or Google DOGAMI Lidar Oregon.
Scenes from the 1997 movie *Total Reality* (F13) were filmed inside the Montgomery Park building.

TREE-HUGGED HYDRANT

Where: NW Thurman between 24th & 25th on the north side of the street

Google Coords 45.535499 -122.701928

Nearby: App 1, #1; App 2, #31-32; Entry C5

OBSCURE · POPULAR

OBSCUR-O-METER

C 2

The Corey is a fire hydrant. Not an ordinary fire hydrant, but rather one in danger of being swallowed whole by an Ash. Swallowed whole *Ripley's Believe-it-or-Not* style. According to Portland Water Bureau records The Corey was installed circa 1925. It took 63 years for the Ash tree to engulf The Corey enough to send him into retirement. City records show that, on December 20, 1988 *"due to a large root around the old hydrant"* a new hydrant, Mueller, was installed a few feet away.

Hurry and go see The Corey before he's tree-hugged into oblivion.

Lucy and Corey

Outer West

CURIOUSER? The World Forestry Center up by the zoo in Washington Park has a cut tree stump that has completely eaten a rifle. There are numerous other examples the world over, including the famed "bicycle-in-the-tree" up at Seattle's Vashon Island (sadly vandalized just months before this writing). Google "Trees growing around things" for a fun world tour.

SWIFTS

Where: 1445 NW 26th Ave at 26th & Pettygrove

Google Coords 45.533212 -122.705978

Nearby: App 1, #1; App 2, #31-32; Entry C5

C3

MAP P. 74

OBSCUR-O-METER

Each and every September, all month long, a googol of Vaux Swifts return to NW Portland's Chapman School to roost in its immense age-old chimney. **This is a BFD in PDX.** "Why?" the uninitiated might ask. "Why would folks bother to gather at dusk on the grassy hillsides surrounding the Chapman School each night of September to watch some birds fly around? Isn't there already a bird on everything in Portland?"

Duh. This is the world's finest swifts-show, a veritable Audubon autobahn of avian acrobatics. Like a tornado in reverse, these Lilliputian birds swirl into a sky-darkening funnel cloud before vortexing en masse downwards into the chimney to roost for the night. **WOW**, to say the least. Nightly, a crowd gathers to watch the spectacle...people from all walks of life...a colorful assemblage of Portland's one

Villainous Cooper's Hawk

or two ethnic groups. Just like at 4th of July fireworks, expect an appreciative crowd oohing and ahhhing over the aerial show. Except...*GASP*...when the dastardly hawks show up and perch on the chimney lip, darkness filling their raptor hearts. Yikes, its hawks vs. vaux, just like a live action *National Geographic* special! Hahaha, listen to the green-leaning families loudly booing any hawk successes. Good fun is sitting near a black-clad group of Goth youth and listening to them root on the dark-hearted hawks whilst the nearby soccer moms seethe with righteous indignation.

Don't forget your camera

Free and Abundant Swift Watch Parking at Montgomery Park
NW 27th & Vaughn

Very limited on-street parking near Chapman Elementary

CURIOUSER? Note: Parking near Chapman can be a bitch. Cars swirl the streets en masse just like the birds above. Poor parking behavior is rampant and the neighborhood is none-too-pleased. Tow trucks park in waiting just like the hawks. Do everyone a favor and park in Montgomery Park's spacious lot and walk the seven blocks after checking out the oddities there (C1), or park at Selco Credit Union at 25th and Thurman and walk the four blocks after checking on Corey (C2).

C 4

BIKE LANE GUYS, REVISITED

Where: 2770 NW Cornell Road

🔷 **Google Coords** ▶ 45.531112 -122.706347

Nearby: App 4, #3

MAP P. 74

OBSCURE ← → POPULAR
OBSCUR-O-METER

Outer West

Our cover photo. Portland's bike lane guys (or bike lane art, or bike lane stencils) are one of the city's quintessentially quirky "Portland-isms."

Portland's modified bike lane guys date back to 1999. We know this because a good citizen named Jim Waigand became enamored with the arsty stencils back in the 2000s and began collecting photos of them and keeping a spreadsheet of all their locations—there were at least a hundred! Jim also wrote a lengthy article about the origins of this quirky PDX art form which was published, oddly enough, in the British bicycling magazine VeloVision in 2003 (available online or on our website). For the article Jim tracked-down and interviewed Todd Roberts, the

Sweeping off the Juggler, just another work day

unlikely Portland Bureau of Trans. employee who started it all. Sure enough, in true PDX fashion, Todd modified some bike stencils as a rogue lark,

Golf Girl
NE 33rd

but soon PBOT supervisors were encouraging their workers to follow Todd's lead and get creative in the bike lanes. Joe Biel, of local Microcosm Publishing, added to the history with a 2006 video called *Martinis in the Bike Lane*. This 11-minute video (available on DVD at Microcosm, or a 6-minute version on YouTube) shows how years later Kirstin Byer and her PBOT crew actually crafted the artsy stencils and then literally melted them onto the streets. In the mid-2000s a FLICKr photo group, *Portland Bike Lane Stencils*, was established and it still (2014) hosts a collection of stencil photos. In 2013 the PDXccentric team ran around tracking down as many of the remaining stencils as we could find. What we sadly found was that due to repaving and general wear and tear over the years, only a few dozen remained. Sadly, by the summer of 2014 when we were nearing the end of writing this book we went to compile a list of our top five and found that almost all of the ones on our list had been paved over in just the last year! Oh, no we thought, better see them before they all are gone.

Note: In this 2015 reprinting of the book I am happy to say that Kirstin and her PBOT team are back at it. Increased interest in the bike guys has encouraged them to get more creative than ever! Here is a list of our current favorites. There are so many now, we will give you ten to go see! Thanks PBOT for bringing fun back to the bike lanes.

SE Water Ave.

N. Broadway

SW Terwilliger Blvd.

Top 10 Bike Guys:
1. Our cover boy, the exquisite unicycle juggler. 2770 NW Cornell Road.
2. Rose Princess N. Broadway & Ross, next to the Moda Center.
3. Fireman NW Naito Pkwy & Ash, across from the fire station.
4. Chicken crossing the road NE Glisan & 43rd.
5. Scuba diver SE Water Ave. & Salmon.
6. Golf gal, with clubs, tee, ball…and even a flagstick up ahead 8448 NE 33rd Ave.
7. Markus Mariota, Heisman trophy winner, NW Naito Pkwy & Couch.
8. Stick horse jockey, SW Terwilliger Blvd & Campus Drive.
9. Transportation hero, N. Vancouver & Russell.

SW 4th & Jefferson

10. Last but not least Portlandia (with artistic influence by PDXccentric and designed to celebrate Lady P's 30th birthday) SW Jefferson between 4th & 5th.

WITCH'S CASTLE

Where: 2999 NW Upshur. From parking walk an easy .8 miles to the ruins.

Google Coords ▶ 45.528612 -122.724489

Nearby: App 2, #31-32

MAP P. 74

OBSCUR-O-METER

The Witch's Castle is Portland's most photogenic ruin. Tucked creekside along a popular Forest Park trail, the rock, moss, steps, window and pointy steeples of this "castle" make it impossible to take a bad photo, even with an Android phone.

2014

The laughs are on you though if, like the nimrods before Google dashed their idiocy, you don't clue-in to the <u>fact</u> that the Witch's Castle was built as a bathroom, not as some haunted dungeon/gallows/Ghostbusters lair. A PDX newcomer might nowadays read, from any of a number of sources, how these ruins were built as a 1930s "Convenience Station" bathroom by Depression-era CCC/WPA workers (this date is wrong—more on this later). This once-grand "station" inconveniently fell to ruin when the calamitous 1962 Columbus Day Storm laid waste to its infrastructure. After that, it was deemed cost prohibitive to get this broken bathroom back up to functioning. Later in the '60s the city removed the roof to decrease the risk of fire hazard.

By the 1980s and '90s civic memory was fading as to exactly what this rock 'n' moss temple was built for. Into this knowledge wasteland eagerly stumbled the nimrods. Nonsense bloomed in Macleay Park to fill-in the information gap. Before Google came along to debunk the myth-makers, some self-appointed ghostbusters had re-purposed the defunct bathroom as some sort of insidious murderer's lair. Somehow they took the classic early-Portland Danford Balch murder case, rearranged the facts, and moved the new myth to this bathroom. Who you gonna call? Hahahaha, check YouTube to see the 'busters chasing ghosts in this toilet! Yeesh, the only ghost you'd find might be that of Thomas Crapper, but even his ghost fled the onslaught of Mensa-deprived Ray Parker Jr. fans.

MACLEAY PARK SHELTER, PORTLAND, OREGON
Ernest F. Tucker, Architect

Architect and Engineer Vol. 106 July 1931

Now, about that CCC/WPA myth:

The CCC began in 1933, the WPA in 1935. Neither of these groups built the bathroom, despite what most every "reliable" source says. The bathroom was built by the City of Portland in 1929, as *Oregonian* articles clearly illustrate. For further proof, after an exhaustive search, Aimee finally found a dated photo of the structure from a 1931 *Architect and Engineer* periodical. Other than one photo owned by local historian Don Nelson (published in *A History of Northwest Portland: From the River to the Hills*) this is the ONLY other photo we've ever seen of the Witch's Castle when it was the Macleay comfort station.

SHELTER BUILT IN PARK

MACLEAY CANYON HAVEN IN INACCESSIBLE PLACE.

Materials Lowered in Basket on Highline; Structure Fits Rustic Setting.

The bureau of parks is just finishing a shelter at the bottom of the ravine in Macleay park. Although only ten minutes' drive from the shopping district of Portland, the site of the building was entirely inaccessible for truck, sled or packhorse, and the materials had to be sent down on a high line especially erected for the purpose.

Pedestrians can reach the spot by steep trails and long flights of steps, but the contractors, Angell & Son,

Oregonian 1-12-30

CURIOUSER? Google Danford Balch murder or go to our blog for links to listen to podcasts from Offbeat Oregon History blog and Kick Ass Oregon History blog.
Find YouTube ghostbusting links on our website.
To see a similar, yet still standing, structure check out the shuttered comfort station at the NW corner of Dunaway Park off SW 6th at Sheridan St. Portland's tallest Douglas Fir tree is along the trail.

WILLAMETTE STONE

Where: 221 NW Skyline Blvd.

 Google Coords ▶ 45.521154 -122.743521

Nearby: App 4, #2

OBSCURE — POPULAR
OBSCUR-O-METER

Outer West

1885 Original

The Willamette Stone is arguably the single most important point in all of the Pacific Northwest. Never heard of it? Oh the shame…but don't feel too alone. Few know of the Willamette Stone and fewer yet have made the effort to visit it, even though the li'l state park surrounding this *Navel of the Northwest** is only a few minutes' drive up Burnside from NW PDX.

What, where, why? In brief, the Willamette Stone is the spot, demarcated in 1851, where all land surveying for the NW began. From this unlikely spot a survey Baseline runs E-W from ocean to Idaho and a Meridian runs N-S from Canada to California. Thus, every piece of real estate in OR/WA, every topo map grid, every arcane "Township and Range" notation of every deed for every business…relates back to the Willamette Stone.

Is Willamette Stone State Park worth your time to visit? Yup, for two strange reasons. The first strange reason is that you can't actually see a damn thing from the Willy Stone. You'd think the "point of initial survey" would sport some far-ranging views to help out the initial surveying. Nope. This point was more "backed-into" than chosen-ahead-of-time. Surveyor Preston first determined the E-W baseline should pass south of the Columbia River. Then, more importantly, he positioned the N-S Meridian so that it would pass chiefly through the most-populous areas of the young Oregon Territory (Willamette Valley and Olympia/Tacoma). Where these two lines intersected became the "Initial Point."

Secondly, a visit to the park will show you the itty-bitty remains of the Willamette Stone surrounded by three

1967 Vandalized

*Historical photos on this page courtesy of Portland City Archives

88

benches and a 9-foot-square concrete slab inlaid with explanatory plaques. Get this: our oh-so important "Navel of the NW" has had quite the sordid history since the "Initial Point" became an engraved rock with a catchy moniker way back in 1885. This original 1885 Willamette Stone was crafted as an engraved monolith (eight inches square), sticking two feet out of the ground. This

Willamette Stone today

monument existed unscathed for 66 years until unholy vandals bonked it with a "heavy hammer" and knocked it in half. A blasphemous outrage worthy of *The Oregonian*'s front page!

The Willamette Stone was repaired and re-mounted in 1956 with the new 9-foot-slab and brass additions, but sadly time and vandals have not been kind. Not only was our Willy knocked apart again in 1967…but finally in 1987 the best bit of the original 1885 obelisk—the engraved four sides—was sheared off completely and STOLEN. Bastards!

State Police Hunting for Vandals After Historic Marker Despoiled

Oregonian 8-13-51

Sheriff Joins Vandal Hunt

Oregonian 8-14-51

Survey Stone Remains, But Top Portion Missing

Oregonian 6-24-67

All we have left now is a meager stone—a mere nubbin of the Willy Stone's historic 2-foot glory. This Willamette Nubbin is such a pittance that it even pools water after a drizzle, forming a Willy Puddle. Damn, somebody somewhere has an 8-inch square hunk of mythic NW heritage. Someone wakes each day to read "Base…Line…Will…Mer" as he/she romances our stone. Which devil did this dastardly deed???

CURIOUSER? * *"Navel of the Northwest"* **was coined by Maynard Drawson for the Willamette Stone in his premier 1973 eccentric guidebook *Treasures of the Oregon Country*.**

TRAIL OF IMPRESSIONS

Where: SW 18th between Yamhill & Jefferson

 Google Coords ▶ 45.521293 -122.690467

Nearby: App 1, #2; App 4, #2-3

OBSCUR-O-METER

C 7

MAP P. 74

Outer West

A curious collection of 15 concrete etchings line the sidewalks of Goose Hollow along SW 18th St. They stretch from Yamhill to Jefferson on both sides of the street. The quirky etchings present a hodge-podge history of the Goose Hollow neighborhood. It makes for a fun walking loop to tour all the etchings trying to decipher the various depictions (exacts words/descriptions are available on our website if you can't make out the 20-year-old etchings). The series of picto-stories was commisioned by TriMet in 1995 when they tore-up 18th Street to install the West Side Light Rail. A submission contest was held amongst neighborhood residents and then a local cartoonist named Matt Wuerker was hired to carve the winning stories into the wet cement of the sidewalks.

THE GOOSE HOLLOW ART WALK MAP

Lincoln High School Fence, Carolyn King

TRI-MET

Each of the 15 etchings has its own backstory, but aside from the Bart Simpson urban myth (C8), our favorite two etchings are the Bud Clark commemorative limerick and the 1951 ski-jumping contest that was held within Civic Stadium (Providence Park).

Bud Clark Limerick: Neighbors wanted to honor Goose Hollow's favorite-son Mayor Bud Clark, and Matt Wuerker came up with the idea of a limerick contest to go along with a cartoon of Bud paddling his canoe down the Willamette. To get the nighborhood's creative juices flowing, Wuerker penned some limericks such as...

"There once was a man from Goose Hollow,
People told him if he ran they would follow,
The campaign was a hoot,
Ivancie got the boot,
and Bud Clark got City Hall and a gavel."

Westside Light Rail Public Art Guide TriMet

Wuerker (right) and Jane Glazer help Bud
Clark (left) judge over 100 entries received
for a limerick contest to commemorate Clark,
local tavern owner and former mayor of
Portland. The limerick winner was Pete Dorn.

This got the ball rolling, and then Wuerker, Bud Clark and poet Jane Glazer chose a winning limerick out of over 100 entries. (See Entry A12)

> *"Whoop Whoop was the curious cheer,*
> *Of a colorful barkeep near here,*
> *This common tax payer, Served two terms as mayor*
> *Then returned to his former career."*

1951 Civic Stadium Ski-Jump: For the 1951 Rose Festival an incredible 135-foot-high ski jump was built above/inside Multnomah Civic Stadium (Providence Park). Block ice was shaved and packed onto the ramps. Ski-jumpers flew so far they smashed into hay bales at the far end of the stadium floor to stop. The spectators gawked at the *smashing* daredevil success.

CURIOUSER? On our website: TriMet's Etching-art brochure. *Oregonian* articles about ski-jump contest.

BART SIMPSON
Who's Your Daddy?

Where: SW 18th & Salmon St.

Google Coords ▶ 45.519727 -122.691553

Nearby: App 1, #2; App 4, #2-3

OBSCUR-O-METER

There's a 2-foot long etching of Bart Simpson in the cement sidewalk on a SW 18th Street just outside the wall surrounding Lincoln High School's track. *Simpsons* creator Matt Groening is, of course, a celebrated alum of Lincoln. On the sidewalk next to the Bart etching it says "Matt Groening" and "Class of '72." Around Portland it seems that the popular urban myth is that Groening himself secretly engraved Bart into the wet cement when TriMet refigured the light rail tracks/sidewalk in 1995.

Don't believe the myth.

Here's the Bart Simpson Myth as portrayed in Portland's popular media: (and there's plenty more online references also)

- ***Oregonian* 5/2012:** "Groening drew and signed a sidewalk portrait of Bart Simpson in wet concrete outside his alma mater…"
- **Wikipedia Kings Hill/SW Salmon:** "*Simpsons* creator Matt Groening etched Bart Simpson into the east sidewalk."
- **GooseHollow.org:** "Matt Groening (creator of *The Simpsons* and graduate of LHS) drew a picture of Bart Simpson in the wet cement after the sidewalk was poured."
- **Portland's Goose Hollow by Tracy Prince:** "Matt Groening, creator of *The Simpsons*, is a famous Lincoln High School graduate. He sketched Bart Simpson in the wet cement of the sidewalk along the west end of the field."
- ***Walking Portland* (A Falcon Guide) by Sybilla Cook:** "The first one is a sketch of Bart Simpson by his creator, Matt Groening, a 1972 graduate of Lincoln High School."

Here's the real story:

Emmy-winning cartoonist Matt didn't draw Bart...nope, instead a Pulitzer-Prize-winning cartoonist also named Matt drew our Bart. Confused? Here's the facts. A freelancing local cartoonist named Matt Wuerker, who had at one time drawn cartoons for the *Willamette Week*, was hired by TriMet in 1995 to create an entire series of sidewalk etchings along the new sidewalks of SW 18th Street (entry C7). These etchings were supposed to celebrate the neighborhood's history...and one of the etchings was to be of Bart Simpson to honor Lincoln High's favorite son, Matt Groening.

MATT WUERKER
I L L U S T R A T O R

INVOICE FOR THE TRAIL OF IMPRESSIONS (#1)
Images completed by September 23, 1995

1.) Bud Clark

2.) Portland Railway Company

3.) Henry Miller

4.) Bart Simpson

5.) Raccoons   5 x $447   = $2,235

Total now due: $2,235.00

For us here at Xccentral the Bart myth seemed unlikely and upon some digging it began to unravel when Aimee unearthed an obscure TriMet art literature pamphlet about these 18th Street etchings— the so-called "Trail of Impressions." One doubt about the origin of the Bart Simpson etching lead to another until Aimee eventually met with Mary Preister, TriMet's Public Art Manager.

Explaining to Mary the online prevalence of the Groening/Bart myth, Mary was quick to pull out a 20-year-old file folder about the Trail of Impressions project and produce the invoice that Matt Wuerker had submitted for etching the Bart and 14 other sidewalk panels. Additional documents in the folder further proved Wuerker the actual etcher, but just to be positive an email was sent to the newly-Pulitzer'd Wuerker who then replied and verified that he did indeed etch the Bart.

Another myth bites the dust, hey, hey...another myth bites the dust.

Wuerker's WW cover, 12-16-98

CURIOUSER? Our website has the TriMet invoices, etc, as well as some other Matt Wuerker works.

And speaking of "who's your daddy?" not many PDX'ers are aware that Matt's dad Homer was a cartoonist for the *Oregonian* in the 1950s. Check our website for a collection of Homer Groening cartoons.

EXPOSE YOURSELF TO CLARK

Where: 1927 SW Jefferson

 Google Coords ▶ **45.518380 -122.693879**

Nearby: App 1, #2; App 4, #2-3

OBSCURE — POPULAR
OBSCUR-O-METER

C 9
MAP P. 74

One magic morning in 1978 a legend was born. Local photographer/ newsman Mike Ryerson schemed with a local barkeep to pose someone "flashing" the naked, controversial, and newly-installed Kvinneakt statue as a promotion for the Venereal Disease Action Council. The willing accomplice was Bud Clark, the devil-may-care owner of the popular Goose Hollow Inn pub. Little did anyone know at the time, but the ensuing "Expose Yourself to Art" poster was soon to become world-famous, selling literally millions of copies.

expose yourself to art™

Even littler did anyone know that Bud Clark, whose irreverent visage was now broadcast the world over, would campaign for Mayor of Portland just six years later...and win. Bud Clark, famed for his mustache, his lederhosen, his rowdy pub, his stand-up canoeing, his *"Whoop, Whoop"* salutations...the same Bud Clark stepped up to run for mayor in 1984 when nobody else would. Few if anyone gave the fun-loving and rarely-serious Bud even an iota of a chance against the entrenched old-guard incumbent Frank Ivancie. Nobody but Bud, that is. Bud took himself seriously and mortgaged his home to kick-off a last-minute low-budget underdog campaign.

Portland 1984 wanted change more than anyone (except Bud) guessed. Bud won the primary in legendary fashion and became the exalted "People's Mayor." His first order of business, *whoop whoop*, was to hold a massive rock concert to raise money to pay back the campaign loans he took out against his house. The Mayor's Ball was a huge hit, the first of eight years of them. The people LOVED Bud. Bud was weird, Bud was mayor...and it was time to say hello to an all-new kind of Portland!

Do ya already know Bud's story and that of *"Expose Yourself to Art"*? If so, good on ya. Too few new Portlanders do. Bud's story should be required reading for PDX citizenry. Google Bud, Wikipedia Bud, read *Willamette Week's* online *"This Bud's for You"* or a 3/2014 *Portland Business Journal* online interview with Bud.

EXPOSE YOURSELF TO CLARK

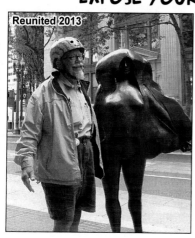

Reunited 2013

OK, now that you've freshened your knowledge of Bud and know how he shines like our own crazy diamond, the next order of business is to go on a downtown "Tour of the Bud" to figuratively (and maybe literally) expose yourself to the Bud Clark mementos scattered about town.

1. **Kvinneakt**, of course (App, 1, #5). She still stands naked to the world kitty-corner from Pioneer Courthouse Square (6th & Morrison), though she did get

continued ➡

moved from her original "Expose" location). Go give our world-famous naked dame a look and maybe a fond fondle to keep her shiny bits shiny.

2. **5th and Washington.** (45.520312 -122.6766540) If you like to play match-'em-up with old photos, this is the original placement for Kvinneakt, just a short 3-block walk from her current location. This is where Bud did the "flash seen 'round the world." Check the background of the poster to match-up the doorway, columns, grown-up trees, and even a plaque…and surely you'll flash at least a smile. (This is also the Alis Volat Propriis building in Entry B9)

3. **Goose Hollow Inn.** Still PDX's best Rueben. You might still run into the legend himself there, though he's long retired from the day-to-day. If you get lucky "flash" him at least a smile.

4. **18th and Jefferson.** Downhill a half block from the Goose Hollow Inn, at 18th and Jefferson on the corner of the sidewalk, resides a fabulous cement engraving of Bud stand-up canoeing and shouting an iconic *"Whoop Whoop"* to the few passersby who chance to look down (Entry C7). The fun way to Expose Yourself to Clark here is simply to lift either your skirt or kilt and perform a little curtsey.

THE PEOPLE OF PORTLAND ARE ITS
GREATEST TREASURE.

PORTLAND'S GREATNESS IS IN THE
LIVABILITY OF ITS NEIGHBORHOODS.
IT IS THE PEOPLE WHO MAKE SURE
THAT PORTLAND IS CLEAN, SAFE,
AND PROSPEROUS. OUR CITY IS A
JEWEL ON THE BANKS OF THE
WILLAMETTE RIVER AND THE
CULTURAL AND TRADING HUB OF
THE COLUMBIA BASIN.

IF PEOPLE HOLD FAST TO THESE
PRIORITIES: FAMILY, BUSINESS,
AND COMMUNITY, AND IF WE ARE
STEADFAST IN PRESERVING THE
QUALITY OF OUR ENVIRONMENT, THEN
PORTLAND WILL REMAIN ONE OF
THE BEST PLACES ON EARTH TO LIVE,
TO PROSPER, AND TO RAISE A NEW
GENERATION TO CARRY ON OUR
TRADITIONS.

J. E. BUD CLARK
CITIZEN MAYOR
1985 THROUGH 1992

5. **Under the Burnside Bridge.** At the Light-Rail stop on First St. (just north of the Skidmore Fountain) you'll find a brass plaque sporting Bud's smiling mug. Undoubtedly more than a few PDXers have stopped to share a Bud with our buddy Bud here...*nudge-nudge-wink-wink.*

6. **Bud Clark Commons.** The Commons is an apartment building catering to homeless folk, kitty-corner from Union Station (655 NW Hoyt). Opened in 2011, this building was named for Bud after for his civil service and the renowned 12-step homeless plan he championed as mayor.

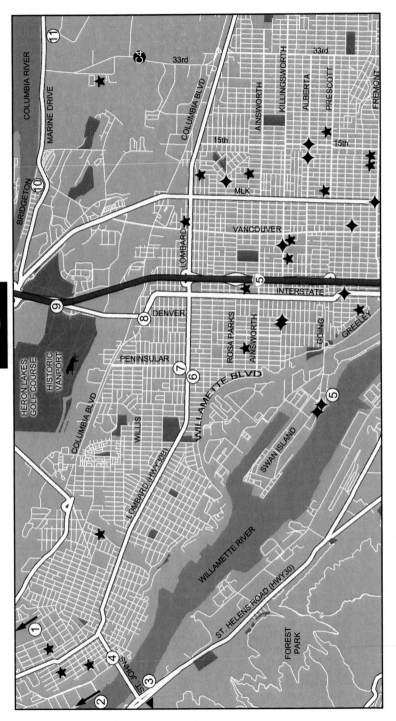

NORTH PORTLAND

APPENDIX KEY

♥ Hot, Not, or Learn-a-lot Statues

♦ Custom Bike Racks

★ Intersection Murals

▲ Viewpoints

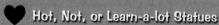
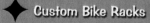

WAPATO JAIL

Where: 14355 N Bybee Lake Ct.

Google Coords ▶ 45.626574 -122.757174

Nearby:

MAP P. 98

OBSCURE — POPULAR
OBSCUR-O-METER

Portland's got a problem. Or, maybe Portland doesn't. Maybe Portland doesn't have enough problems, and that's the problem. What if the city built a huge new prison and Portland doesn't have enough criminals to fill it?

Wapato Jail is a fancy new 10-year-old prison built in 2004 with buckets of taxpayer money... just when criminals fled Portland en masse for richer thieving grounds. Seems that maybe criminals got wise to the fact that Portland's retirees were young and poor rather than old and rich. Thus, Portland has a state-of-the-art never-opened jail, mostly because there just isn't enough crime anymore. Sorry though, here in guidebook land we're not gonna try to tell you about the City Commission's trials and tribulations over the Wapato debacle. Even the *LA Times* bashed Wapato in a 2006 article titled, hahaha, "This Jail Takes No Prisoners," quoting the sheriff at-the-time, "We held a ceremony, cut the ribbon—then locked the doors." If you're curious, then get your Google on.

Instead of the controversial history, we'd rather dwell on the upside of empty jails. Hooray for Hollywood, PDX style. Yup, the ever-empty Wapato is high on every local location-scout's HOT list because not only can the pristine prison portray an actual inmate-free jail, it can also double as

Unused jail beds

an office building, medical center, crime lab, high-tech lab...or... you name it. And even better yet, from Hollywood's perspective, not only is the state-of-the-art facility flexible but it can also be had for just

Photo *Oregon Live*

Grimm Season 2 ep 11

pennies a day courtesy of a snafu in Portland's prison-funding measure. It's like Hollywood and TV have a sort of "get *into* jail free card." Ha, reality at Wapato isn't grim...it's *Grimm*!

Since the homeless have stated their opposition to moving to Wapato because it is too far from "city services," there seem few ideas that have the "Leverage" to remedy Wapato's empty nest syndrome. The Brothers McMenamin were summoned for a savior role, but $58 million seemed even a bit too much for them.

Hmmmm...maybe the city could move the GasCo Building (D3) over there and operate the entire site as a multi-facility film studio. Too bad the Lovejoy Ramp got demolished, as it would have been nice there too, but we could still move the leftover Lovejoy Columns possibly (B4). Ideas anyone?

Leverage Season 3 ep 1

CURIOUSER? Besides being featured in *Grimm*, *Leverage* and *Portlandia* Wapato was also used as the office building in the movie *Spiral* (F16). Also, John Breen of *The Auteur* (F17) starred in a movie *Cell Count* filmed entirely at Wapato.

SAUVIE ISLAND UFO

Where: Sauvie Island, Collins Beach first parking entrance

Google Coords ▶ 45.784370 -122.785320

Nearby: ...

OBSCURE / POPULAR

OBSCUR-O-METER

North Portland

UNIDENTIFIED FLYING OBJECT?
UNIDENTIFIED FLOATING OBJECT?

For close to two decades a peculiar "ship" has been wrecked high ashore in the middle of Sauvie Island's popular nude beach. Every so often people bounce queries around the web as to the origin and purpose of this strange craft. A popular guess is *"some sort of lifeboat"*… but the naked truth is rarely ascertained. The mystery ship is round and flying-saucer-like, so what the hell is it—shipwreck or saucerwreck?

On Halloween 2012 KOIN's Tim Becker went out to have a look, interview a wildlife ranger, and put the nude beach UFO on TV. Facts were few and conjecture ruled the land. The newscast's mysterious implications stimulated interest, mostly by UFO nutters, but also by a few

KOIN's 10/31/12 newscast

TIM BECKER
SAUVIE ISLAND

4:18 58°

The Oregonian

Democrats in Senate to support war cutoff

Reconciliation call rebuffed by Hanoi

Oregonian 1/5/1973

FLOATING SAUCER — Richard Ensign's $10,000, 15-ton sailboat may look like a flying saucer, but to his pleasure, it floats. Ensign, who spent two years building the unusual boat, says it was all an experiment and he doesn't yet know what will come of it. The boat made its way through the locks on the Willamette River at West Linn Thursday on its way to Astoria and the Pacific Ocean. Story on Page 11.

people actually connected with the ship, namely the boat's creator and its first passenger. Little-known to the legion of people who have watched the original "mysterious implications" newscast is that Becker did a follow-up news story on the Sauvie UFO-boat a few months later. Becker surprisingly discovered that the mystery-ship had been featured on the front page of the *Oregonian* on 1/5/73 as it embarked on its maiden voyage. Becker also found a woman who had been a passenger on the boat's inaugural voyage as a 4-year-old child those 40 years ago. For the follow-up video she brought along a treasure-trove of '70s photos from the boat's voyages and shared them with the camera as she and Becker reminisced at the site of the wrecked boat. In a nutshell, the wrecked boat was a tri-hulled cement-covered self-righting sailboat designed for up to twelve people to live aboard. Overall, Becker did an excellent journalistic job of digging-up the truth behind all the initial mystery.

North Portland

BUT, strangely enough, the detailed follow-up newscast got "lost" in the YouTube and it's only been viewed about 1,538 times, compared to the original newscast's 336,193 views (10-6-2014). Since the videos don't link-up on YouTube, most Portland peeps only get the stripped-down "mysterious" version of the Sauvie UFO-boat, instead of the whole skinny. If you want to know the full story you'll have to watch both videos.

TO SEE THE SHIPWRECK:
Sauvie Island beaches require a $7 daily parking pass, easily obtained at the mini-mart at the base of the Sauvie Island bridge. After driving all the way up the island and past the clothed-beach access parking spaces, the road turns to gravel. You want to stop and park at the third signed nude-beach entrance point on the gravel road. Once out on the beach the wreck is up in the trees just a couple hundred yards to the right (upriver).

CURIOUSER? Links to Becker's videos on our website as well as screenshot captures of the 1970s photos shown in the videos...plus the *Oregonian*'s front-page story from 1973.

This shipwreck can be seen in the background of the final "climax" scene in *The Auteur* (F17).

A GLIS HALF FULL?

D 3

Where: Roughly between St. Helens Rd to the Willamette & from NW Vaughn St. to the St. Johns Bridge

Google Coords ▶ **45.579563 -122.762578**

MAP P. 98

Nearby: App 4, #1

OBSCURE — POPULAR

OBSCUR-O-METER

Guilds **L**ake **I**ndustrial **S**anctuary. Who would have guessed?

Guilds Lake (C1) a century ago was a shallow wetlands lake alive with birds and beavers and probably every other critter that most cities nowadays pay truckloads to save. Not Portland. Fast forward Guilds Lake a hundred years and it has become a sanctuary…but not the sanctuary you'd expect.

Map 1: Guild's Lake Industrial Sanctuary

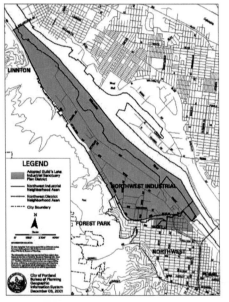

Imagine a busy industrial part of the city…trains clanging, trucks roaring, contractors scurrying, toxins <u>seeping</u>…Mother Nature frowning. Most cities would call this "renewal district." Not Portland. Portland calls it a sanctuary district. Guilds Lake Industrial Sanctuary. Only in a city <u>so</u> abounding in green…hemmed-in by forested parks, rivers, wildlife refuge, protected waterways, greenways, every-which-ways…a city where manholes become parks and a paved-over stream is celebrated…a city where industry is elbowed aside to make room for "a place for young people to retire"…only in a city like Portland can the politicians take a stand against civic encroachment and enact a sanctuary for <u>industry</u>. All hail the GLIS!

"Oh give me no homes,
Where no buffalo roam,
Where no deer nor antelope play,
Where seldom is heard,
A leisurely word,
And the skies are kept smoky all day"

from "Home on the GLIS," 2013

Illustration by Jason Reynolds

Most of the year the GLIS huffs and puffs along without incident, safe and secure from do-gooders trying to somehow preserve or park-ify it. But controversy rocked the GLIS in 2013 when NW Natural announced their intention to raze the derelict 1913 GasCo building in order to continue a superfund clean-up. "Whoa, hey…wait" some good citizens responded. Seems like a plethora of citizens are enamored with the GasCo gothic derelict building, some even referring to it as "an industrial cathedral." The problem though is that the former office building is itself an asbestos hazard and also sits atop a toxic plume of superfund soup. NW Natural needs to and wants to get on with the necessary Superfund clean-up while the funds are available and the getting-on is good. Some citizens though cry foul and want the quasi-beloved building "saved" to become some sort of park or McMenamins or something. Yikes, trouble in industrial paradise…Portland style. Isn't the very purpose of the GLIS though to keep these very sorts of PDX greenie do-goodings away from this rare sanctuary for industry? A Portland sanctuary under siege…Oct. 2015, demolition begins.

CURIOUSER? Wikipedia: **Northwest Industrial, Portland Oregon.** Google and download the entire 91-page PDF for the Industrial Sanctuary plan. Fun!

ST. JOHNS BRIDGE/ CATHEDRAL PARK

Where: N Edison St & Pittsburg Ave

 Google Coords ▶ 45.588661 -122.757288

Nearby: App 3 #1-4; App 4, #1

D 4

MAP P. 98

OBSCURE · POPULAR

OBSCUR-O-METER

North Portland

Photo Portland City Archives

The 1931 St. Johns Bridge is without a doubt Portland's most photogenic and iconic bridge. Add the stunning array of Cathedral Park's gothic bridge supports under the northern end and you've got a can't-miss orgy of megapixels. The St. Johns Bridge might have the best above/below combo of any bridge in the nation. It's near impossible to take a bad photo of <u>any</u> part of the St. Johns Bridge. (Also see App 4)

Atop the Bridge. A walk out to the center of the span is a must (best walked from the St. Johns side, parking under the bridge). On a clear day can you see the four nearby snow-capped volcanic peaks (for out-of-towners Mt. Hood is the pointy one rising over East Portland, Mt. Adams is sighted directly down the length of the bridge, and flat-topped Mt. St. Helens is left (north) of the bridge with the tip of humped Mt. Rainier just to its left). Whoa, not only four volcanoes to complement the gothic spires 'n' wires, you can also see the arcing Fremont Bridge and our two downtown skyscrapers, Big Pink and Wells Fargo Center.

And, not only that, but you can also get lucky atop the St. Johns Bridge. On each of the four portal walkways which skirt the four bridge supports, the decorative lamp holders feature 4-leaf clovers. Hmmm, did bridge designer David Steinman surmise that these walkway portals would be a good place for you and your honey to have a little shamrock shake as trucks rumble past?

Shamrock

106

For a great photo-op of the entire bridge-span 'n' spires, walk all the way across the bridge and turn left (south) for 90 more yards to find the Ridge Trail staircase at the cement wall. Head up the steps for just a couple hundred feet and you'll get a fantastic view of the bridge from a wooden walkway.

Cathedral Park. It'll surprise you. Who'd guess the underside of a bridge could be this shutter-snappish? This odyssey of arch-ways is a favorite of movies and *Portlandia/Grimm* TV shows. Nuff said. Go. Parking underneath the bridge is best.

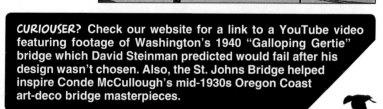

CURIOUSER? Check our website for a link to a YouTube video featuring footage of Washington's 1940 "Galloping Gertie" bridge which David Steinman predicted would fail after his design wasn't chosen. Also, the St. Johns Bridge helped inspire Conde McCullough's mid-1930s Oregon Coast art-deco bridge masterpieces.

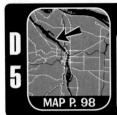

LINDBERGH'S BEACH

Where: 4299 N Port Center Way

Google Coords ▶ 45.553552 -122.698145

Nearby: App 2, #4-8, App 3, #7

D 5

OBSCURE — POPULAR
OBSCUR-O-METER

Lindbergh's Beach on Swan Island is Portland's best city beach. Of course, just like all the local Columbia/Willamette beaches, the sand here doesn't appear until around July 4th when the river recedes from its annual June high water. Surprisingly, given how unknown it is, Lindbergh's has plenty of invitingly soft sand sloping into the Willamette as well as nice views of the Fremont Bridge, Portland skyline, and Forest Park.

Slough Biscuit's favorite swimming spot

The reason the PDXccentric staff calls this little-known stretch of sand "Lindbergh's" is two-fold. First-fold, the name is meant to purposely confuse everyone. For example, let's say you are playing a game of Giant Jenga at the Triple Nickel and you begin raving about the fun sunset skinny-dipping your posse did at Lindbergh's last weekend. See? The geeks waiting to play Jenga next won't have a clue what Lindbergh's is. They'll just keep texting, slightly embarrassed that they've never been skinny-dipping. If you had said "Swan Island Beach," then you betcha they'd have Google Earth open on their Galaxy 5's faster than you could say "Star Trek re-enactment...how about next weekend?"

Second-fold, the name isn't just random—we didn't just choose the name of a smelly cheese or something like that to keep the masses away. Charles Lindbergh did actually land on Swan Island on Sept 14, 1927 to officially open Portland's very first Municipal Airport. Yup, Lindy himself, newly-minted international hero from his solo flight across the Atlantic just four months prior, landed the *Spirit of St. Louis* on Swan Island to a hero's welcome (before his Portland landing he had first taken a sightseeing

Lindy on Swan Island

flight up the Columbia River Gorge where he daringly swooped <u>under</u> the Bridge of the Gods!) The Lindy visit was a **HUGE** PDX event, definitely the biggest aeronautical happening since Silas Christofferson flew off the Multnomah Hotel rooftop in 1912 (B11).

(**NOTE:** there are two stretches of Lindbergh's, accessed on either side of the Port of Portland HQ building. **BUT**, summer 2014 saw the demolition of the Port HQ... and we have no idea what's planned for the area and the parking. You'll have to see for yourself and be flexible. The downriver access-point may still have the excellent interpretive sign that detailed all the local history with neat photos.)

Oregonian 9/14/1927

TODAY IS THE DAY

Photo Portland City Archives, 1935

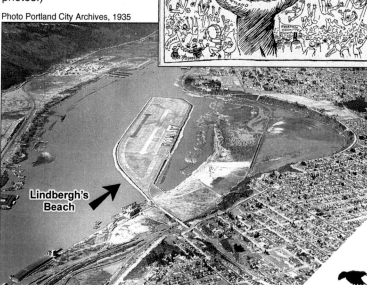
Lindbergh's Beach

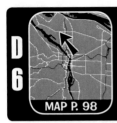

D 6

MAP P. 98

ONE TREE TO RULE THEM ALL

Where: Emerald St. alley 3226 N. Lombard

⊕ Google Coords ▶ 45.576582 -122.699912

Nearby: App 3, #5-6 &9

OBSCURE ◀ POPULAR

OBSCUR-O-METER

Size does matter.

PORTLAND HERITAGE TREE
GIANT SEQUOIA
Sequoiadendron giganteum
Designated by Portland City Council 2005

North Portland

Portland has lots of trees. Lots of big trees, lots of Heritage Trees, an entire vast Forest Park of trees, even a tree in the world's smallest park (A8). None are as impressive as one unlikely gigantic Goliath—the one tree to rule them all. This behemoth grows where you wouldn't even consider looking for the biggest of the big—just steps off of Lombard Street in North Portland along a semi-paved alley. This tree is a spectacle amongst Portland's trees. A tree truly living up to the name *Giant Sequoia*.

The jaw-drop impressiveness of this tree is not its vertical, but rather it's horizontal. As Aimee sometimes remarks, it's not the tree's length that matters…it's the width. The Heritage Tree program lists this tree's circumference (at chest level) as 29.5 feet. Divide that by π and you get a whole lotta diameter. You need to bring a couple of friends just to give this tree a noticeable hug. And, as if a ten-foot-wide trunk at chest level isn't enough WOW, this Sequoiadendron Giganteum flares-out dramatically at its base, busting through the backyard fence to rupture the alley.

Say no more…go see…you'll like.

CURIOUSER? Portland's tallest tree is a Doug Fir in Forest Park residing just 100 steps downstream from the Witch's Castle (C5). The 2nd most impressive of Portland's Giant Sequoias grows on the flat park area between Mt. Tabor's two reservoirs, near the bottom of the steep staircase.

PORTLAND HORSE PROJECT

Where: Rings are all over Portland (our #1
    3011 N. Lombard)

Google Coords ▶ 45.577217 -122.697553

Nearby: App 3, #5-6 &9

OBSCUR-O-METER

North Portland

Many century-old curbs along Portland's older streets feature iron rings fastened into the cement. These rings were meant to tie-up horses and carriages in the day before the automobile began its reign. For the past century most of these curbside rings did nothing but rust and remind in-the-know Portlanders of a bygone era.

SWI's first horse 9/24/05 (note string lariat)

Photo Courtesy of Scott Wayne Indiana

In 2005 though, into the ring stepped a spirited lad named Scott Wayne Indiana. S.W.I., intrigued by all the historic mementos he saw on so many Portland streets, sometimes had the great notion that the horse rings should once again have horses tied to them. Toy horses. No reason other than to make himself and others smile at the quirky playfulness of a tethered toy. SWI named his eccentric offerings "The Horse Ring Project"…and he soon inspired a small legion of like-minded citizens to attach toy horses all over the city. Portland soon fell in love with the equine eccentricity of it all.

Scott Wayne Indiana has since moved to NYC for one of those job thingies, but the Horse Project lives on…though only a shadow of its late-2000s heyday. In 2011 a short film documentary was made in celebration

Green Zebra

of SWI and the story of the horse rings. Google *"It's a Ring Thing: The Portland Horse Project"* or link through the film's webpage. Scott Wayne also maintains a website and a Facebook page under *Portland Horse Project*. Thus, if you see a li'l horse on a ring, take a photo and upload it to the Facebook page to share it with everyone.

Barley Mill SE Hawthorne

Google "Portland Horse rings" to see a veritable herd of photos from the past decade.

We here at Xccentral of course love the toy ponies. The trouble with the little tethered ponies is that they often go missing often as soon as someone tells us where they saw one. Drat...which dastardly rustler has such blackness at heart to snip the wire and make-off with the "neigh"-borhood icon? So...people know <u>about</u> the tethered toy horses, but it's pretty hard to actually tell someone where they can see one for themselves.

Fear not though kind reader. Aimee has been in contact with a few spots around North Portland who are committed to keeping horses on their rings for all to see and smile. Aimee also guarantees that you will love buying yourself a Dollar-Store horse and wiring it to the curb. If you yourself are committed to keeping a toy horse on a particular ring, let us know and we can put it on our website to share the fun with others. Here are three likely spots to get your horse-ring fix:

Attaching your own horse is funner than you'd think!

In North Portland:
1. **N. Peninsular and Lombard**
2. **In front of the Overlook Veterinary Hospital 2009 N. Killingsworth Ave. Killingsworth and Denver**
3. **In front of the Naked Sheep Knit Shop, 2142 N. Killingsworth Ave. Killingsworth and Gay St.**

PAUL BUNYAN'S BABES

Where: 8411 N. Denver

Google Coords ▶ 45.583836 -122.686600

Nearby: App 3, #5-6 & 9

MAP P. 98

OBSCUR-O-METER

OBSCURE — POPULAR

Everyone knows the giant Paul Bunyan that presides over the north end of Kenton. But who knows about the four bigger-than-life blue hooves that hide across the street—the hooves of Babe, the giant blue ox? Paul's erection was way back in '59 by the good citizens of Kenton in order to celebrate Oregon's centennial. But what of Paul's companion? What happened to Babe the ox? Well, it seems that it took 45 years for Babe to be reunited with Paul.

Paul stood proudly his first 5 years on the corner, greeting every interstate traveler coming down the 'pike from the north, until the 1964 completion of I-5 (the Minnesota Freeway). The new freeway bypassed Interstate Ave (and its span of neon-lit motels) leaving lonesome Paul without any travelers to greet anymore (the old

Kentonites Build Big Paul

Oregonian, 5-20-1959

Hwy 99 interstate came down Interstate Ave., then over the Steel Bridge and down Harbor Drive before exiting Portland towards Corvallis). For a brief time in 1972 Paul's smile returned when Raquel Welch arrived in town to film *Kansas City Bomber*. Raquel stayed at the old Thunderbird Hotel and spent some time filming at the "not-yet-famous" Kenton Club in

Wink-wink

her curve-hugging knit dress, turning the place quickly into the "World-Famous" Kenton Club. Va-va-voom! Surely Raquel gave Paul a wink or two in response to his wecloming grin.

Paul's lonely years continued until George opened the "Dancin' Bare" strip club across the street in 1990. Sure Paul missed his Babe, but now he could at least watch the comings and goings of George's babes. Paul's grin returned, especially when the Bare girls hosted their annual car wash.

North Portland

114

BABE'S IN THE WOODS?

For 45 years Paul had wondered where his ox had gotten off to. Had she wandered off into the woods, gone on the hoof, so to speak? Well, in 2004 she finally came back to his side, though only in spirit. Between 2002-2004 TriMet brought Light-Rail up Interstate Ave. As part of the work they re-oriented the north endpoint of Denver Ave., necessitating the moving of Paul. Paul used to stand in a small plaza which is nowadays where the Denver Ave. crosswalk is. He moved SE just a bit and got a new circular base, while the new intersection left an empty triangle of sidewalk across the street. In TriMet's artsy fashion they hired local artist Brian Borello to design four blue hooves for the new sidewalk triange to represent Paul's companion Babe. Also in TriMet fashion, they don't really tell anyone that these new blue bench-like structures have a story behind them. Babe got back! Yippee, thought Paul, grin ever wider, now he's surrounded by babes.

Now that you know about the bigger-than-life hooves, maybe head over to Kenton and see Paul's grin from a hoof-seat. Paul's eyes look skyward most of the time, but if you sit on the hooves and watch closely, we swear that when the Dancin' Bare gals come out for a smoke Paul's eyes dart downward and his grin widens a trifle. Go see for yourself…and then maybe hop off Babe and hoof it over to the Kenton Club to have a drink where Paul's second-favorite babe once cavorted.

CURIOUSER? On our website is a link to Roadside America's "A catalogue of Bunyans."

Use the Google Earth history-timer to go back to 2001 to see Paul at the old Interstate/Denver corner.

Paul makes his sole Hollywood appearance in *Down and Out with the Dolls* (F14).

Thanks to Carye Bye (the Museum Lady) for mentioning the hooves in her *Hidden Portland* booklet. The authors had both driven by hundreds of times without ever noticing Babe's hooves.

VESTIGES OF VANPORT

Where: 10000 N Expo Road

 Google Coords ▶ 45.596142 -122.685737

Nearby:

OBSCUR-O-METER

Vanport was a city and is now an enigma. A slice of Portlanders know a great deal about this 1940s "instant city," while the rest of the citizenry doesn't seem to know diddley about Vanport and the cataclysmic tragedy that befell it. This guidebook isn't going to even attempt to summarize the well-told tale. Google "Vanport" and you'll quickly get up to speed, especially if you also spend a few minutes on some YouTube/Vimeo vids. Yup, the 6-year saga of America's biggest-ever public works project, wiped out in mere minutes by the flooding Columbia River, is indeed must-know PDX IQ.

Vanport City

Theater

Portland City Archives

Google will indeed gush you a flood of Vanport pix…but what Google won't gush is "what's left of Vanport nowadays?" This is the question that always tickled us here at PDXccentral. Most "experts" we questioned said, "Nope, nothing left…all gone…now just Portland International Raceway (PIR), Heron Lakes Golf Course, and a dog park." Nobody seemed to know of any remnants or ruins. Hmmm…we didn't like that answer.

Turns out there is one woman who knows different. Terri Johnson is a 27-year Vanport resident...and that's saying something, given that Vanport only existed for 5 years. Terri is the resident caretaker of PIR and has lived on the PIR (former Vanport) grounds for the past 27 years (as of 2014). Terri <u>knows</u> Vanport. During Aimee's search for vanished Vanport she was eventually steered towards Terri... and...score! Upon introduction and questioning Terri simply said," get in the truck and I'll show you the only real remnant of Vanport." A quick drive down the winding backroads to the western edge of the PIR racetrack and Voilá, Terri stands on and points out what was the angling cement floor of Vanport's celebrated 750-seat theater. There's not too much to actually see other than the bolt-hole patterns from the seats. Terri recounts how the cement used to angle down like an amphitheater bowl, but the "bowl" was filled-in about 25 years ago to beautify and lawsuit-proof the PIR grounds. Hmmm...someday when Portland wins the lottery, or maybe when Mike McMenamin is elected mayor...maybe there'll be money to dig-out this theater-bowl and revive it as an outdoor amphitheater. Hmmm, don't hold your breath.

Honestly, there's not much to see at this theater spot. But if you're our kind of curious, here's the deets: first you need to drive into PIR past the Delta Park/Vanport TriMet station when races aren't going on. Drive around the open side of the toll-booth gates and go to the racetrack parking lot. You need to pull-up to the small 3-story PIR office and ask permission to go back on the grounds. The PIR folks are nice and they'll point you in the direction or answer questions. Basically, from the office drive west behind all the grandstands then through a gate as the road becomes gravel, keep going to the far corner of the racetrack and where the road bends right, stop at the large grassy area and look for the Vanport vestige under the power lines at the SW corner of the grassy area (map on our website).

Theater prior to Memorial Day Flood 5-30-48

Remains of Theater

continued ➡

More interesting than the theater site, is Terri's hard-earned treasure-trove of Vanport relics that she has personally collected in her 27 years at **Vanport.**

By "collected" we mean that she has poked around and dug in the mud with screwdriver and shovel in a tireless search for evidence of Vanport's flood-strewn remnants. Terri's keen eye and dedication has unearthed scads of stuffs—all sorts of housewares and ceramics, US Navy flashlights and whistles, toy trucks, cars etc. etc. Some neat finds are a 1930s Baby Brownie Kodak camera, a 1940s transistor radio, a toy bank full of pre-1948 pennies…as well as a 1947 Oregon license plate and a 1942 South Dakota plate. Quite a collection of Vanished Vanport, all dug out of the mud all around the grounds. This is

the only such collection that exists anywhere! Alas…Terri's collection is not on public display—it's all over her house….BUT…

But, strangely enough, when TriMet extended the light-rail to Delta Park/Vanport in 2002, they got wind of Terri's collection and decided to **immortalize the artifacts at the light-rail stop**. TriMet and artist Linda Wysong borrowed a bunch of Terri's choice artifacts and had a metal sculptor cast them in bronze to create four eight-foot sections of railing. However, true to TriMet form, they don't tell anyone that these relic-railings are actual remnants of Vanport rather than just a collection of old junk. Nobody at the light-rail stop gives them any notice…and why would they since TriMet doesn't tell you anything about them. Some particularly neat things to look for on the sections of railing are a toy Greyhound bus

Relic Railing

(where you can see the greyhound-dog emblem), the "USN 1944" Navy whistle, one-half of the pair of binoculars, a perfume bottle that looks like a grenade, and the easily-readable "Sloan's Liniment" bottles (pix of all these and more on our website).

Portland City Archives

Vanport Flood 5-30-48

Also, a glance over the relic-railings will reveal yet more TriMet art-riddles. Below the rail platform you'll see some rusting geometric forms. What TriMet doesn't tell you is that what these pyramids are intended to represent are the floating rooftops of the flood-ravaged apartment buildings, which actually did float over to this exact corner of the flooded city. Who knew? Lastly, on the rail platforms be sure to look out for the Vanport-map mosaic (regrettably oriented 90° the wrong direction). Also down by the rusty rooftops look for the drain spout also crafted from Terri's treasures.

CURIOUSER? Video on Vanport by Brian Van Peski http://vimeo.com/851414
Book on "Vanport" by Manley Maber

SPEED BUMP GLYPHS

Where: N Bridgeton Road

Google Coords ▶ 45.600979 -122.655567

Nearby: Entry C4; App 3, #8

OBSCURE — POPULAR
OBSCUR-O-METER

N. Michigan St.

Speed bumps are the newest canvas for Portland's wacky PBOT painters. Inner-neighborhood speed bumps, or in the parlance of Portland Bureau of Trans., "traffic-calming devices," have taken-over from bike-lane guys as PBOT's outlet for creativity (C4). Truth-be-told, the crack team here at PDXcentral only recently stumbled upon this new form of PDXpression while on the search for the last of the fast-disappearing bike-lane art guys. Hooray, every day a new way for PDX to be gay (not the LGBT *gay*, but rather *merry*, like a prankster). Woohoo, now you can excitedly rally your imaginary girlfriend, "Hey, let's rent a Zip Car and scout-out some new glyphs on the traffic-calming devices." "Hold on," she'd imaginarily reply, "wait till I finish knitting these yarn bombs. Maybe you can grab some toy horses in case there are any sidewalk horse rings by the traffic calmers."

Um, right. What other city besides PDX decorates their speed bumps? Not a one! Everywhere else we go speed bumps are a traffic-slowing annoyance, but here in PDX you can now be annoyed and entertained at once. Gotta love it—why should those bike-lane painters have all the fun and get all the GLORY anyhow? If you were a speed bump painter wouldn't you get bored of painting dull chevron patterns and, ugh, wide straight stripes? Yessiree then…let's get creative with colorful little animals, nautical themes….suns, snowflakes, bats and geese in yellow, blue, green and white…and hey, why not, even our city flag now and again.

NW Cornell Road

Bridgeton Road boat-themed glyphs

Traffic-calming glyphs are bunched on just a few stretches of PDX roads (as of 2015).

Here's where:

- Along Bridgeton Rd off Marine Drive there are eight different boat-themed stencils on eight consecutive speed bumps (409 NE Bridgeton Rd).

- In NW, heading west on Lovejoy the road bends uphill and becomes Cornell. After the bend the second speed bump has a couple of geese on it, and within the next mile (to the tunnel turn-around) there are four more glyph-bumps, our favorites being the smiling sun and the snowflake that bookend our book-cover bike-lane unicycle-juggler (2646 NW Cornell Rd).

- Along N. Michigan St. between Fremont and Alberta there are seven speed bumps decorated with whimsical whatnots, including a nice miniature city flag (4134 N. Michigan Ave).

- On NE Klickitat there are stencils at 63rd and 38th.

121

LIGHT RAIL COYOTE

Where: TriMet Max light rail stop at Portland Airport.

 Google Coords ▶ 45.587505 -122.593055

Nearby:

OBSCURE · POPULAR
OBSCUR-O-METER

Once upon a time: Back in 2002 a coyote was seen running around the runways of PDX, as they are wont to do. This coyote was different though. Perhaps a bit more wily. Chased by Port of Portland security, the wily coyote bolted from the runways, scampered over the railroad tracks and leapt...into fame! Specifically, he leapt onto an empty MAX light-rail train, hopped onto a seat and curled up for his clever getaway. Drats though, the security man (Port employee Dennis Maxwell) caught up with him. Dennis, sensing no menace from this wily rascal, whipped out his camera. One quick photo for a man, one giant leap for coyote-kind. The photo made the front page of the *Oregonian*, the nightly TV newscasts...and thus, the legend of Portland's light-rail coyote was born.

DENNIS MAXWELL/PORT OF PORTLAND

Relaxing on MAX: A coyote, hoping to make a getaway from Portland International Airport on Wednesday, hopped a light-rail train but didn't get a ride. Crews said the coyote walked onto a train when a guard boarded for a security check. The critter was captured by the airport's wildlife specialists, then released outside the security fence.

Oregonian 2/15/2002

Twice upon a time: This particular light-rail coyote wasn't done with his fifteen minutes of fame quite yet. In late 2002 an all-girl punk-rock trio left Olympia WA, via the exit that they had named their band after (Sleater-Kinney) and moved their gig down the road to Portland. These three raucous riot grrrls, arriving in Portland, were charmed to the MAX by the image they saw of the local rails-riding rascal. Inspired, they penned a now-classic homage-to-Portland anthem named "Light-Rail Coyote."

"Out on the edge of town
Where airfield runs water down
Coyote crosses the tracks
And hops on the Light-rail MAX"

Thrice upon a time: In 2006 Sleater-Kinney broke up, but the legend and spirit of light-rail coyote lived on. Though Sleater-Kinney was done, singer/guitarist Carrie Brownstein wasn't done with Portland. Her new gig was with a guy named Fred, borrowing their name from our beloved trident-wielding copper goddess.

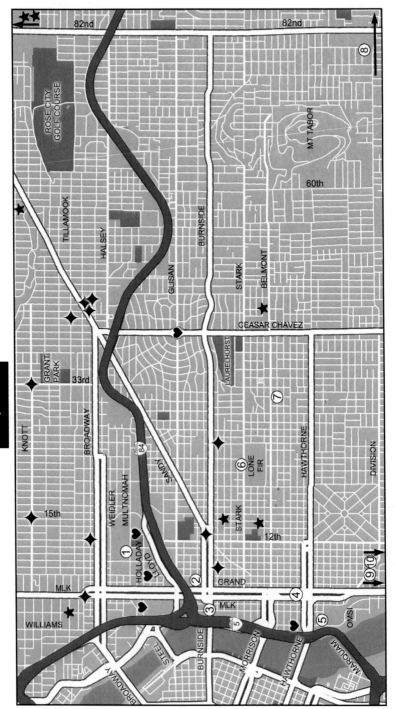

EASTSIDE

E

APPENDIX KEY

♥ Hot, Not, or Learn-a-lot Statues

◆ Custom Bike Racks

★ Intersection Murals

▲ Viewpoints

VEXED IN THE BIKE LANE

E 1

MAP P. 124

Where: On Multnomah St. between 6th & 16th Aves.

Google Coords 45.531537 -122.649652

Nearby: App 1, #14-16; App 2, #13

OBSCURE   POPULAR

OBSCUR-O-METER

The Timber's Army flying Portland's colors

Vexillology is the study of flags. Local vexillologists are vexed as to why Portlanders don't seem to know that we have a beautiful city flag, except maybe the Timbers Army. Oddly, other than a scattering of downtown flag poles, the BEST place to see Portland's colors is on Multnomah Street along the south side of Lloyd Center. But, along Multnomah you don't look skywards to see the flag as you might think, but rather you need to look down. The Portland flag was emblazoned onto the asphalt of the bike lane no less than eight times in the ten blocks from 6th to 16th streets. Weird. Neat!

Eastside

Of course you've seen the bike lane art stencils (C4), and you may have seen some of the newer speed-bump glyphs (D10), but this series of colorful full-size flags is known mostly only to the few bike commuters who salute them on their daily pedal. Hurry and go take a look at these colorful street arts because they seem to be aging and flaking-off fast.

The man behind these creations was PBOT's Ross Swanson. He was tasked in 2012 to add some flare to the newly-created bike-lane buffer, and, whoa, he outdid himself! This buffer is part of PBOT's "road diet" initiative where car lanes shrink and bike lanes expand. Yet to be determined is whether this "road diet" is more Atkins, South Beach, or Paleo. What we know is we really like these vexing flags.

> *Adopted:* 4 September 2002 (official), originally adopted 1969
>
> DESIGN: *There is designated an official flag for the City to be known as the City Flag and described as follows: The standard size measures 5 feet in length by 3 feet in height. The background shall be green, symbolizing the forests and our green City. The design includes a four-pointed directional star, formed by the vertical and horizontal intersection of counterchanged blue stripes, symbolizing our rivers. The blue stripes are paralleled with yellow stripes, symbolizing agriculture and commerce. The yellow stripes are separated from the green background and the blue river stripes by white lines called fimbriations. The white central star is positioned slightly left of center, toward the staff end of the flag, called the hoist.* (Ordinance 176874, amending Portland's *City Code* Section 1.06.010.)

CURIOUSER? The flag depicted here is the latest iteration of our city flag. Hit our website to see the flag that flew from 1970 until its 2002 redesign.
Also, check BikePortland's "NE Multnomah St" blog post.

STARK'S VACUUM MUSEUM

Where: 107 NE Grand Ave. at Couch

Google Coords ▶ 45.523772 -122.660813

Nearby: App 2, #23-24, App 3, #20-22

E 2

MAP P. 124

OBSCURE — POPULAR

OBSCUR-O-METER

This is Portland's only museum that's meant to suck. Hahaha…literally—everything in this museum sucks! Stark's Vacuum is a vast vacuum cleaner showroom in which, tucked-away in a corner of all this vacuum vastness, is the famed free Vacuum Museum. If a vacuum museum sounds like an odd "attraction," well, you're right, it is. But, chances are, these thirty steps through a century and a half of suction history will make you chuckle more than you expect.

Vacuum "technology," so to speak, has made laughable leaps and bounds since the pre-electricity 1890s. Hahaha, if you think vacuuming sucks now, you should see how your great grandma had to do it. The back corner of the museum area features pump-action bellows-contraptions that must have required exhausting pumping and contortions to suck up some meager microns of dirt. Other hard-to-believe pneumatic gadgets required two people to operate, looking more like scuba apparatus than "time-saving devices." Strangely enough, all these devices were considered huge leaps forward for housewives in time-savings and leisure-having. One iconic 1910 model sports a colorful emblem proclaiming Vacuna

Eastside

128

as the *Goddess of Leisure*. Who knew vacuuming was a leisure activity or that it had a goddess? (Haha, we thought guidebook writing made you a god/goddess of leisure).

Another don't-miss chuckle is the Filter Queen adaptor kit in the back row of the museum. Here you can see how to adapt your vacuum into a vibrator or hair dryer so you can continue to "enjoy the appliance" in all your new leisure time. The depictions of the man using the vibrator all over his body are hilarious! Get this—the text with the drawings reads, *Gentle soothing vibrations gives you that "Great to be alive feeling".*

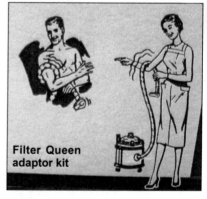

Filter Queen adaptor kit

The Stark's Vacuum Museum definitely delivers that "great to be alive feeling" also, even if you only have time for a short 10-15 minute visit. Check it out—everything in it sucks, but it doesn't suck.

CURIOUSER? Google Vacuna "Goddess of Leisure"... and maybe buy her Roman coin on Ebay.

BURNSIDE PROJECT

Where: 35 NE 2nd

Google Coords 45.523129 -122.663662

Nearby: App 2, #23-24; App 3, #20-22; Entry B15

MAP P. 124

OBSCURE — POPULAR
OBSCUR-O-METER

E 3

Burnside is Legend.

The Burnside skate park story is legendary to skaters throughout the world. In brief, rogue skateboarders began constructing an illegal skate park under the Burnside Bridge in late 1990, and then somehow won over the city and mayor to receive official approval. Closer to home, the story of the Burnside skate park is part of our own urban legend…and true to Portland form, Burnside has a place in the PDX "unlikely legends" pantheon with the defeat of the Mt. Hood Freeway, Harbor Drive removal, Pioneer Courthouse Square, Bud Clark's election, Vortex concert, etc etc. The Burnside is another rogue citizen-initiated idea becoming a civics lesson for the rest of the country…as well as a pilgrimage spot for skaters everywhere. Golf has its Augusta, NASCAR has its Daytona, horse-racing has its Kentucky Derby, surfing has its Pipeline…and Skateboarding has Burnside.

Funny thing though is that people outside of Portland are often more familiar with the Burnside story than many who live here. If you're a long-time local, yet don't know the details of the Burnside legend, well, you're

Eastside

Dogpercy on Imgur.com

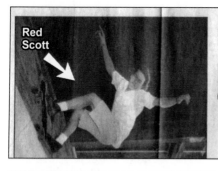

Red Scott

Life's a grind

Concrete kingdom with rebel flair lures skateboarders far and wide

By BILL DONAHUE
Special writer, The Oregonian

Oregonian 8/2/1991

Skate: Ingenuity, muscle and sweat build a park

not alone. This legend lived in the underground, "under the bridge" so to speak. Until just the past few years, learning of the Burnside legend wasn't all that easy unless you were in the sk8 community. Not so anymore, thanks to the web. Now you'll find plenty of online lists heaping on praise, like Bombdecks', *"This legendary location…is easily the most acclaimed skate park on the planet."* We Xccentrix aren't skaters, and thus feel unworthy of recounting the legend of Burnside. We're just here to try to help you know where to look. Until this legend gets the <u>book treatment it deserves</u> the deets are on the web.

CITY OF

PORTLAND, OREGON

OFFICE OF PUBLIC AFFAIRS

Eastside

June 15, 1992

MEMORANDUM

TO: Mayor J.E. Bud Clark
                Commissioner Earl Blumenauer
                Commissioner Dick Bogle
                Commissioner Gretchen Kafoury

FROM: Commissioner Mike Lindberg

RE: Council Calendar No. 1153
                Resolution in Support of Skateboard Area

continued ➡

On the Web...

- **www.BurnsideProject.blogspot.com** hosts a fantastic historical overview written by Burnside pioneer Chuck Willis. <u>Fucking</u> <u>Awesome!!</u>

- *Full Tilt Boogie*, is a Burnside documentary made by Burnside pioneer Chris Bredesen. It was released onto Vimeo.com circa 2012/13. Interviews, footage, old photos, politics, and perspectives. <u>Epic</u>!

- **Burnside Project** on Facebook has all kinds of interesting stuffs hidden on its timeline.

- OPB did an *Oregon Field Guide* episode **"Skateboarding"** in 2006. Great props to Burnside from outside the skater world.

- ESPN chimed-in with a piece on Burnside in 2010.

- Superb photo gallery of early Burnside by Dogpercy on Imgur.com. Google "Dogpercy Burnside"

(There are links to all of the above on our website.)

Burnside Ashtray

HOLLYWOOD LOVES BURNSIDE

Burnside is Hollywood's darling when it comes to movies filmed in Portland. Here's the notable appearances we've found thus far (Check film appendix for more details, with screengrabs on our website).

***Ironheart* (1992 – filmed in 1990)** The skate park doesn't appear in this almost-unknown Portland Kung-fu movie. What does appear are scenes shot under the Burnside Bridge just months before Red Scott and the gang started building the first bits of the park. In the movie there are shoot-outs, exploding cars, and mayhem, all where just months later, the skatepark began to take shape.

***Free Willy* (1993)** The almost-new Burnside makes a brief cameo near the film's start, sandwiched between scenes shot at Pioneer Courthouse Square and under the Morrison Bridge.

Angelina hangin' on the hip

***Foxfire* (1996)** Whoa, young Angelina Jolie parties with her gang of girl-power rogues in the skate park. Not only do the girls monkey around while skaters bust it, the girls actually tag the Punk Wall with "Foxfire Burn and Burn", while Angelina reclines on the famed hip. Angelina then skates topless (ha, just kidding).

***Down & Out with the Dolls* (2001)** The band's adventurous drummer is watching her hapless boyfriend try to skate Burnside when she falls in lust with a local lesbian.

Down and Out

***The Hunted* (2003)** In the PDX action-packed 15-minute sequence, Tommy Lee Jones gazes over the Burnside for a brief moment, sandwiched between him running through Schrunk Plaza and then standing atop the Keller Fountain.

***Paranoid Park* (2007)** The Burnside Skatepark co-stars in the movie, playing "Paranoid Park." Sadly, the footage for the legendary co-star dwindles after minute 20. Great to see Sage and Chuck in the credits.

Untraceable

***Untraceable* (2008)** A skater finds out his dad is being tortured over the internet while skating at Burnside.

KIDD'S TOY MUSEUM

Where: 1301 SE Grand Ave

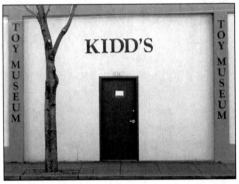

Google Coords ▶ 45.513547 -122.660878

Nearby: App 1, #13; App 3, #20-22

OBSCURE — POPULAR
OBSCUR-0-METER

Kidd's Toy Museum is a bit of an odd duck, definitely a longtime fixture of "weird" Portland. On the outside all you see is a nondescript door with a peephole with an unremarkable "Kidd's Toy Museum" painted down the corner of the building. No windows at all, and thus no visuals of the toys 'n' oddities contained therein. Knock on the locked door and you'll be let in for free. The outsides may seem weird if you're expecting a kid's museum…but this ain't no kid's museum, it's Kidd's museum.

> WE THINK YOU WILL ENJOY THIS MUSEUM MORE IF YOU FIRST WATCH SOME VIDEO SHOWING VINTAGE BANKS IN ACTION. SINCE AT KIDD'S THEY ARE IN LOCKED CASES. YOUTUBE "STECKBECK MECHANICAL BANK."

All toys are in glass cases

Once inside what you'll find is a sort of windowless vault containing two rooms of wall-to-wall glass-enclosed shelves displaying Frank Kidd's AMAZING lifetime collection of vintage toys, banks and collectibles. This is probably the best public display of its kind in the world. The "vault" moniker is apt. These toys are a historical treasure trove and thus, you cannot touch or interact with them, but rather only look. Many of these toys are worth more than their weight in gold (Chuck Palahniuk in *Fugitives and Refugees* details one worth 360k in 2003 dollars!) Other than the toys' sheer value, you'll also be treated to a rather jaw-dropping dose of racism involved in toy bank history. Expect to see all kinds of banks painted in garish bigoted blackface. If you are overly sensitive to racism, then Kidd's Toy Museum won't be your cup of tea.

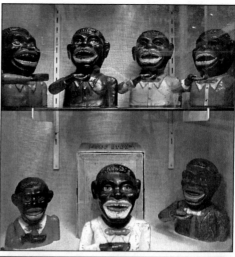

But, the blackface banks are only a small proportion of the entire collection. There's all kinds of other toys too such as fire trucks, cars, sports figures, dolls, as well as other historic collectibles like antique locks. Straight ahead on entering the museum you'll also see a surprising display of

artifacts from Coon Chicken Inn, a PDX Sandy Blvd institution which kept its oft-protested grinning Blackface entrance opened until 1949 (at 5474 NE Sandy Blvd, now home to Clyde's Prime Rib).

Eastside

Freedman's Bank

A bank worth more than the gold you could fill it with!

CURIOUSER? Part of Frank's collection on display at the museum is the Freedman's Bank, the most valuable toy bank in the world. You can see one in action 15 seconds into the Steckbeck video mentioned above. Also good fun is a review of Kidd's Toy Museum at www.roadsideamerica.com.

GHOST RAMPS OF PORTLAND'S PAST

Where: At SE Water Ave. & Clay

Google Coords 45.511369 -122.666692

Nearby: App 1, #13

Portland is haunted by ghostly freeway ramps, but they're friendly ghosts. These so-called "ramp stubs" jut-out from many of our elevated freeway curves but quickly end, perched high and dry over an abyss of fabulous local history. Strangely enough, especially to newcomers who have yet to learn the saga of the Mt Hood Freeway, these "ghost ramps" whisper to us a reminder about a dire past/future that was averted as Portland began its progressively-planned urban renaissance.

Portland City Archives

Not yet heard of the Mt Hood Freeway? Then you should put down this lowly guidebook and get online so you can read/watch some well-written accounts of this legendary PDX saga. We here at Xccentral don't want to re-hash a story that is told so well by others—we're not worthy. In a nutshell though, if you don't have immediate internet access but are "ramped-up" to see some ghosts...the Mt Hood Freeway was a planned freeway heading east from the Marquam Bridge that was snuffed-out by Mayor Neil Goldschmidt and his progressive allies in the early '70s, but not before cleverly keeping all the federal monies for the proposed freeway here in Portland to begin funding other local transit options, namely the beginning of our now-famed Light Rail. Once the Mt Hood was killed, other planned freeways were cancelled too. REALLY, this story is a MUST-KNOW PDX classic!

Here's where to source it online:

Brief version: Willamette Week's 3/9/2005 "Highway to Hell" by Bob Young. Sweet and to-the-point. "If there was one event that defined Portland in the past 25 years, it was the killing of the Mt Hood Freeway."

Brief w/pix: MtHoodFreeway@blogspot.com. Good summation by historian Jeff, with excellent timeline and photos. "Portlanders took an important first step in curbing cars in favor of public transportation."

Detailed: Portland Mercury's 9/24/2009 "Dead Freeway Society" by Sarah Mirk. Great perspectives!

Exhaustive: Val Ballestrem's 100-page PSU Master's Thesis "In the Shadow of a Concrete Forest" available at Archive.org. Brilliant detailed and exhaustive narrative, with sources listed.

Video: "The Defeat of the Mt Hood Freeway" www.StreetFilms.org. Wonderful 12-minute examination.

Since this is a guidebook, not a history book (though we're sometimes confused), we want to tell you where to go see some of these friendly ghost ramps.

I-5 southbound connection to Mt Hood Freeway

OMSI parking

MADISON ST

Never-built southbound on-ramp to Marquam Bridge

Northbound I-5 ramp onto I-405

Southbound I-5 ramp onto I-405

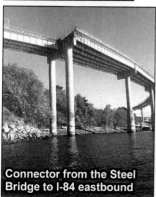

Connector from the Steel Bridge to I-84 eastbound

Cloverleaf's on/off of the Hawthorne Bridge to Harbor Drive

Eastside

CURIOUSER? For some sexy ghost-ramp video action, check out the R-rated music video for the Handsome Furs' song *What About Us*. Not only does it feature nudity, sex, and dance under the Fremont Bridge, it also ends with a ghost ramp finale.

STARK STREET MILESTONES

Where: Along SE Stark starting at 24th to 257th

Google Coords ▶ **45.519261 -122.642109**

Nearby: App1, #17; App 2, #22-23; App 3, #20-22

MAP P. 124

OBSCUR-O-METER

The Stark St. mileposts, or literally "milestones", are the kind of local oddities that are well-known to a handful of PDX history geeks, yet virtually unknown to Portlanders who actually have jobs (hahaha, what a knee-slapper, huh?!). Get this…a series of engraved mileposts, dating to sometime the 1870s, stand sentinel as some of Portland's oldest civic artifacts. These mysterious milestones were emplaced along Stark St to mark the distance eastwards along the Willamette Baseline (C6) from the original 1866 Multnomah County Courthouse. The exact history of the Stark milestones has been debated since at least 1958 when the *Oregon Journal* ran a lengthy examination of them. And, amazingly enough, 56 years later the exact history of the markers still puzzles the internet-enabled local history savants. Aimee gave it her best shot to "solve" the mystery, using her keen Xccentric-toned modern sleuthing techniques…but alas, to no avail. And thus, we need to bow to the original bloggers who alerted us to these mystery-stones and refer you to their writings: blogger Jeff (StarkStreetMarkers@blogspot) and blogger Cyclotram (Milestone P2). As well as those detailed blog posts, our website has historic newspaper articles from both 1958 and 1971…and also more recent articles about some of the stories behind some of the historic mileposts. Some of these stones have neat preservation legacies behind them, as some were literally "saved from the scrap heap."

What's fun is

taking a drive up Stark and trying to locate the nine that still exist out of the original fifteen that spanned the miles eastwards from the Willamette to the Sandy River. To make this outing even funner, shown at right are photos of the remaining mileposts but with the engraved numeral blacked-out (each post has a P then a numeral,

Look what Scott and Moe found in these bushes

"P" being for Portland). Youre "job" is to match each marker numeral with the photo of its post. The first is done. P2 graces the support wall of Lone Fir Cemetery near 23rd Ave. Start there, zero your odometer and head east young man. Stop your car and park at appropriate distances from P2 and get looking! (Note, P5 is tricky as Stark swerves and goes all couplet/

one-way as you wind around Mt. Tabor, but get out and look for P5 near 78th Ave). The others are fairly obvious as long as you are a clever milestoner and zero your odometer at P2. Be safe (maybe you should have a safety meeting before heading out as a group).

Match 'em Up Milestones

P2
P4
P5
P6
P7
P11
P12
P13
P14

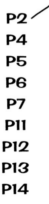

SUNNYSIDE PIAZZA

Where: SE 33rd & Yamhill

Google Coords ▶ 45.515743 -122.630936

Nearby: App 1, #17

OBSCURE — POPULAR
OBSCUR-O-METER

Sunnyside Sunflower

Eastside

Sunnyside Piazza is Portland's second oldest street intersection mural, dating to 2001 (App 3). This giant intersection-spanning sunflower has been studied, examined, polled and counted by all sorts of professional urban studiers. The studies seem to conclude that people are less depressed just living near the Sunnyside sunflower, almost as if the street paint exudes vitamin D. We here at Xccentral have our own theories why people are happier at Sunnyside Piazza. Maybe it's because math is in the air…and on the street! Yes, math. While the S.P. is a painted intersection similar to the other 25 around PDX, the S.P. is the only math-centric intersection art. Perhaps math is the key to happiness. Who knew?

No other intersection art will "spiral" you into a Google-info mind-boggle moreso than Sunnyside's sunflower. The key to unlock the puzzle of life, the universe, and everything is a sequence. The Fibonacci sequence to be precise. 1,1,2,3,5,8,13,21,34, etc etc. Sunnyside Piazza, though appearing a colorful sunflower, is really a famed mathematical sequence painted and tiled upon the intersection. Confused yet? Get your Google on…from nautilus shells to Hurricane Katrina…if you don't know the golden "meaning" of Fibonacci, then sit down at one of the Piazza's benches with your smartphone and get Googling. Yup, Google Image "Fibonacci" and sunflowers will surge forth, accompanied by friends nautilus, pinecone, and pineapple.

Fibonacci tiles

Fibonacci in nature

Now, back in the analog world, be sure to check out the Piazza's kiosk where you'll find that the nutty Sunnyside neighbors have tiled both the Fibonacci number sequence and the numerical representation of the mythic number "phi" on the kiosk walls. Yay, math gone crazy! For more traffic-stopping fun you can walk the sunflower circumference to count the crisscrossing Fibonacci spiral arms (usually 13 one way and 21 the other). Easier to count, (especially if there's a mad traffic jam of similarly spellbound math nutters), are the spiral arms on the metal sidewalk trellis (8 and 5). For folks not too keen on all this enriching math fun, you might just check-in with the *"Fit or Fugly"* Fibonacci iPhone app that'll tell you how perfect your face might be.

Overall, hands down, Sunnyside Piazza is PDX's best learn-more-than-you-wanted-to neighborhood art stop. Yay Math!

Eastside

Phi Φ

CURIOUSER? Who would've known that the designers behind Pioneer Courthouse Square were also Fibonacci fans? Check out the PCS Starbucks pillars for nautilus shells, sunflower spirals...and more! (A1) One of the PCSq designers also designed the Vietnam Memorial up in Washington Park—guess what shape it is?

KELLY BUTTE FORTRESS

Where: 103rd Street. Park at locked gate and walk 300 yards uphill.

Google Coords ▶ 45.500842 -122.556699

Nearby: App 3, #25

OBSCUR-O-METER

Kelly Butte Natural Area is an unassuming forested hill rising just off of I-205 at Division St. Just like neighboring Mt. Tabor and Rocky Butte, Kelly is one of the Boring Lava Field cinder cones. Just like Mt. Tabor and Rocky Butte, Kelly is a city park. Unlike its brethren cinder cones though, Kelly Butte harbors a darkened secret...a filled-in war-room bunker constructed in

Building the hatch in '55

Oregon Journal photo

1955 when the menace of the Red Scare haunted Portland. The Russians had bombs aimed our way and the local plan was for city bureaucrats to escape the impending nuclear annihilation by retreating to the newly-built Kelly Butte Civil Defense Fortress. From there the city leaders would control the dire situation and hold Armageddon at bay.

The Civil Defense concept was a big deal throughout the country in the mid-'50s, and Portland led the nation in its preparedness to escape the imminent Soviet bombing. In 1955 the top of Kelly Butte was hollowed-out and a thick-walled Quonset-hut-shaped bunker was cemented into the hole, then filled-over with dirt. In 1956 Portland staged a successful drill called

"Operation Greenlight" in which much of the downtown was evacuated, simulating an imminent Soviet air strike. *Operation Greenlight* was such a Civil Defense success that in 1957 CBS came to Portland to film a Civil Defense documentary about the evacuation called *"A Day Called X."* This 27-minute documentary, starring the citizens of Portland, including Mayor

Eastside

Terry Schrunk, is super neat to watch on YouTube—it's sort of our own *"War of the Worlds"* with print on the screen telling viewers that **"AN ATTACK IS NOT TAKING PLACE."** (For PDX history geeks, note at minute 2 the old Morrison Street Bridge, with the new Morrison under construction. Cars evacuate over Old Mo at minute 15).

Nowadays there's not much to see atop Kelly Butte except for some corners of the bunker building and two parking lots with a remnant stairway between them. The bunker was basically abandoned by the city in about 1999, whence vandals and homeless moved in to ruin it. In 2006 the 1955 transmission tower was removed and the bunker completely sealed-off with dirt and back-filled. A walk around the parking lots and atop the bunker site is still possible, but you're likely to find more homeless camps than anything else. Expect an eerie/spooky no-man's land sort of feeling. Various user-trails zig-zag atop the butte and over to the new Kelly Butte underground water tank site.

CBS's *"A Day Called X"*

AN ATTACK IS NOT TAKING PLACE

KOIN CBS

Eastside

CURIOUSER? **Digital citizen "Blogger Jeff" has compiled the best Kelly Butte historic rundown, at KellyButteUnderground@ blogspot.com. Then, be sure to check out his links to his other blog KellyButteBunker@blogspot.com where you can see pix of the 1974-1994 use of the bunker as a 911 call center, then the 2006 pix of its dereliction. Whoa, Henk Pander's "Palmyra" mural was far-out!**

MAP P. 124

WILLAMETTE METEORITE

Where: 821 Willamette Falls Dr., West Linn

 45.347070 -122.674616

Nearby:

OBSCURE — POPULAR
OBSCUR-O-METER

E 9

The Willamette Meteorite, prior to 1902, was perched upon a hillside in present-day West Linn. Most meteorites sit in a hole where they land—but not this one. Many a meteor may have meandered farther through space, but **no meteorite has taken a more eccentric journey on the surface of the earth than the Willamette Meteorite.** Many a meteorite have been moved from their earthly landing spots—often with museum destinations in mind. But the Willamette Meteorite is the sole record-sized meteorite that was moved around by Mother Nature before being re-relocated into a museum. The key fact, the key bit of evidence that unlocks the strange saga of the Willamette Meteorite was that the huge meteorite was perched on the West Linn hillside in the company of a whole bunch of white quartz rocks. A-Ha!

Here's the tale:

The currently accepted theory has our meteorite landing sometime in the Ice Age, on the glacial ice northwards of Idaho. This ice sheet "flowed" south, carrying whatever laid upon it for a ride. This same ice sheet was the one that was repeatedly blocking the Clark Fork River to dam up vast Glacial Lake Missoula,

Meteorite being moved to the 1905 Lewis and Clark Expo

which then periodically burst, unleashing the biblical-proportion floods that scoured eastern Washington and gorged-out the Columbia River Gorge. These same iceberg-laden floodwaters filled the Willamette Valley to about...well, to about the elevation where the meteorite was found thousands of years later. Yup, not only did the meteorite land on the Ice Age glacier, it then rode the glacier some miles into Idaho to become part of an ice dam, and then when the ice dam burst the meteorite rode inside an iceberg all the way from Idaho to West Linn. Whoa, maybe the world's weirdest erratic!

Fast forward the geologic clock to 1902, when an enterprising chap named Ellis Hughes "discovers" the 15-ton hunk of metal <u>near</u> his West Linn property. (Local Indians had known and revered the meteorite for centuries as "Tamonowas"). Hughes, deducing that metal hunk was in fact a meteorite, set out to move it from his neighbor's property onto his own.

Eastside

144

Oregonian 10-31-1903

He built a massive cart and had his forlorn horse walk circles around a capstan to drag the meteorite .75 miles onto his property…where he then began charging people a quarter to see it. Unfortunately for ole Ellis, one of his visitors was the lawyer for the neighboring property—the Oregon Iron Company—who then sued Hughes for possession of the meteorite, since evidently Hughes had moved it from their property. The Oregon Supreme Court ruled in favor of Oregon Iron and the meteorite then took another cart ride to the company HQ. Oregon Iron then decided to display their space rock at the 1905 Lewis and Clark Exposition, so then it traveled down the Willamette on a barge to the fairgrounds. From the Expo a philanthropist

Museum photo, 1950s

purchased the meteorite and gifted it to New York's Museum of Natural History. The meteorite was loaded onto a train car for the cross-country journey to its new home…where it still resides today. Quite the earthly journey, huh? It rode on a glacier, an iceberg, a cart or two, a barge, and finally a train. Like Jerry sings, "What a long strange trip it's been."

Eastside

Nowadays the best way to get to know our regrettably long-gone space friend is to visit small Fields Bridge Park along the Tualatin River in West Linn. There you'll find a superbly-crafted interpretive path along the creek bank with a plethora of signs telling the meteorite's fabulous story.

1/5 sized replica
Fields Bridge
Park

The trail ends at a miniature exact replica of the meteorite, allowing you to see and feel the strange erosion/rust sculpting the meteorite suffered on West Linn's wet hillside. (The meteorite's original spot is on private property just 1.4 miles and 280 vertical feet above this little replica). This park and paved trail, just minutes off Hwy 205, are definitely worth the drive!!

THE O.C. O-E VERTICAL STREET

Where: In Oregon City just off Main Street on 7th Ave.

 Google Coords ▶ 45.357223 -122.607887

Nearby:

E10

MAP P. 124

OBSCUR-O-METER
OBSCURE — POPULAR

Riddle: *What do you get when you ride a quirky elevator up a vertical street?*

Oregon City is more steeped in history than eccentricity…except for the gotta-see-to-believe Outdoor Elevator (O-E). The "OC" is where The Oregon Trail ended, becoming the industrial/commercial hub of the growing Oregon Territory. The OC was flying with its own wings before Portland even had any stumps (B9). The main reason for the OC's place in Oregon's history is Willamette Falls. These huge horseshoe-shaped waterfalls span the entire width of the Willamette

Willamette Falls

River just a stone's throw from downtown. Even though the falls have been modified and tamed by 170 years of industry, they are still quite a sight to behold (our favorite way to visit the falls is to paddle upstream in the low-flow late summer from Clackamette Riverside Park). If you are interested in a concise history of how Portland beat out the OC to become today's dominant city, check out Eugene Snyder's *"Stumptown Triumphant"* from a local library.

1915 Elevator

Anyhow, the semi-famous OC O-E was originally built in 1915, but has undergone many-a-modernization since. The reason the elevator exists is because the OC is a split-level town. Big industry and downtown businesses on the lower level while residential is on the upper level. The OC forefathers evidently got tired of the daily trudge up the stairway so they threw-down for a torturously slow water-powered elevator. The elevator proved so popular that the city soon replaced it with a faster and well-lit electric elevator. Seems nobody liked the dark 'vator.

Eastside

So, is it worth a trip to the OC just to ride up and down on the short "vertical street", even if it is the **only vertical street in America?** (Oh c'mon, I know you're already reserving your Zip Car.) YES, the OC O-E is eccentric with a capital E, made all the more odd by the attendants who sit inside the elevator every day to make sure…to make sure what??? To make sure you know how to press "up" when you're down, or "down" when you're up? Hmmm, methinks you might be able to self-manage this choice. There must be a good civic reason, but regardless, try to suppress your smirk when you get in and merrily announce "up please."

But wait, don't stop reading yet, cuz we're only now getting to the <u>really</u> quirky part. In the tunnels approaching the elevator, as well as in the wonderful view plaza at the top, are surely the most eccentric O-Ccentric elevator construction photos known to man. Each printed photo is actually "then and now" time-travel wizardry. These so-called "Lenticular"

prints travel your eyes and brain through a space/time continuum as you walk by them. Don't believe us—go see!

And finally, to answer the opening riddle; a ride up the OC O-E, up America's only vertical street, will surely give you a "vertical smile."

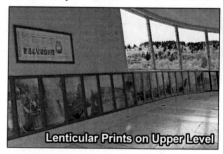

Lenticular Prints on Upper Level

CURIOUSER? For extra fun, from the top of the O-E you can stroll a half-mile south along the McLoughlin Promenade to see the view out over Willamette Falls…or just 100 yards northwards is the "Father of Oregon" McLoughlin House.

The city website has a fun concise history of the 'vator's contentious history.

On Amazon Instant Video for only $1.99 you can watch the 1962 "Route 66" TV episode "Across Walnuts and Wine" to see the boys ride the elevator, cross the original Conde McCullough OC bridge, as well as cavorting all over the OC. This is solid OG OC TV, unlike that latter California show.

F1	1972	Kansas City Bomber
F2	1977	First Love
F3	1982	Unhinged
F4	1989	Drugstore Cowboy
F5	1991	My Own Private Idaho
F6	1993	Body of Evidence
F7	1993	Free Willy
F8	1993	The Temp
F9	1993	Ironheart
F10	1993	Hear No Evil
F11	1993	Brainsmasher
F12	1996	Foxfire
F13	1997	Total Reality
F14	2001	Down and Out with the Dolls
F15	2003	The Hunted
F16	2007	Spiral
F17	2008	The Auteur
F18	2010	Untraceable
F19	2010	Cold Weather
F20	2012	Gone

Films

Portland as FLICK

Our listing of Portland-shot films is the most up-to-date and accurate of its kind. We KNOW because we searched everywhere for a detailed list of Portland-centered films that would give scene-locations, but, frustratingly, we just couldn't find one. Thus, we decided to make the very list that we had been searching for. There are lists on the web such as at OregonFilm.org that list films shot in Oregon with a mention of the main city or filming area, but never any details about exact filming locations or even how much of the movie was shot in Portland. Was it just one scene, or the whole thing?

What we ended up doing was watching 80-100 supposedly "Portland" movies, of which about 80 had recognizable Portland scenes. Movie Madness was a godsend with their huge DVD/VHS inventory, but the web, YouTube, Netflix, Amazon, and even eBay were all needed to find the obscurest-of-obscure. Of the 80 movies we found some Portland in, we've culled this unwieldy herd to a Top-20 that we are featuring here in *PDXccentric* as our Portland as FLICK collection. These 20 are the Portland cream of the crop. There is no perfect way to choose how Portland-centric a movie is. We chose our Top-20 on a subjective scale using approximately 2.5 variable factors to make our decisions. The first and main factor was how many RECOGNIZABLE locations are used in the particular movie. The second and lesser factor was how engaging the movie was to watch, from the perspective of a Portlander (if you're not a Portlander, then most of our Top-20 are not nearly as interesting, since you'd recognize very little…and most of the movies aren't major hits or box-office successes). The third factor is our "special sauce"—our personal fudge-factor to move some movies onto or off of our Top-20 for our own hard-to-pin-down reasoning. Choosing the top movies was easy, but deciding on the bottom few, which to include and which to leave-off, was difficult.

Here are a couple of examples to help illustrate our criteria. Take Mr. Holland's Opus—a great movie that was filmed entirely in Portland, but is mostly unrecognizable to most locals because it was set mostly inside Grant High School, or in outside scenes using tight-focus to exclude any recognizable background. Thus, it fails the "PDX-centric-ness" recognizability test, even though it is a 100% PDX movie. On the other hand, lesser-known films such as Old Joy and Zero Effect fall off the Portland as FLICK Top-20 list because, though each features lots of recognizable PDX, neither measured up to even a 2-out-of-5 on our watchability scale. We would be pained to tell you to watch these films— they are PDX-centric, just not Top-20 material. Other movie such as Feast of Love, Paranoid Park, and Little Blue Pill just didn't make the list because we had to choose just 20 and the axe had to fall somewhere. Overall, most of our Top-20 aren't very "good" movies, and most are almost unknown. Our version of "good" is PDX recognizability, not critical or box-office success. Truth-be-told, more than half the movies on the list are terrible, but their inherent Portland-ness makes them fun to watch regardless.

Ok, so by now you've glanced at our Top-20 list, as well as our Bottom-60. In the pages that follow we give you an intro for each movie to whet your appetite, then a breakdown of the exact shooting locations and the minute they begin within the movie. We chose to dissect the locations that had actual filming done on site, rather than drive-by or aerial skyline shots of the city. We attempted to locate all the major scenes, such as the drugstore break-ins in *Cowboy*, Angelina Jolie atop the Broadway Bridge or in the Burnside Skatepark in *Foxfire*, or when an exploding car hurtled off the Hawthorne Bridge in *Hear No Evil*. We feel that our level-of-detail for our Top-20 is unique. Nowhere else can you find this level of detail for PDX-based films. Knowing where the filming was done, in spots you can recognize, makes even a tepid movie fun to watch. And, to be honest, there's no way we could make our lists this detailed without MAJOR help from the web. Google Earth and street view are a godsend for this. Huge props also the online *Oregonian* archive where we could find "back in the day" news accounts of movie-shooting. Different blogs, fan sites and IMDB chipped-in with some nuggets too. Overall, even though watching many of the Bottom-60 was extremely painful, every movie was like a mini treasure-hunt for us, like movie-location geo-cacheing...and when we stumbled on movies as fun as *Ironheart* and *Unhinged* with no prior expectations...oh how fun!

PoR+LaND as FLICK at Movie Madness

Team PDXccentric is super excited to team-up with Mike Clark's Movie Madness Video and More store to help raise your PDX-film IQ. For those not already acquainted with the iconic and eccentric Movie Madness store on SE Belmont, well then you're in for an unexpected treat. Movie Madness isn't your run-of-the-mill video store filled with New Releases, Box-office hits, and disinterested employees. Oh no. Movie Madness is an eccentric PDX institution all by itself, worthy of inclusion in this guidebook even if they weren't teaming with us to promote the Top-20 PoR+LaND as FLICK movies. Movie Madness is a local legend, the creation of longtime film fanatic Mike Clark who has crafted his store to reflect his passion for all things film. Movie Madness is a movie-memorabilia showroom with huge glass cases filled with Mike's lifetime collection of film costumes, props, and artifacts. Expect to see the famed bar of soap from *Fight Club*, and Julie Andrews' dress from *The Sound of Music*, the ear from *Blue Velvet*, Barbra Streisand's negligee, and the Tom Hanks' watch from *Castaway*... and...and...MORE!

What you'll now also find, near the front counter, is a display rack filled with the PDXccentric Portland as FLICK Top-20 movies. No other store on the planet has as complete a collection of Portland movies as Movie Madness—not even close! Of course everyone knows that the DVD/video business has changed radically in the past decade. But here is a local shop that goes all-out to entertain you and provide a showcase for something like Portland as FLICK. So, shop local we say and Keep Portland Weird... keep Portland good!

And Movie Madness doesn't only feature the Top-20. Mike and his staff are so passionate that they've assembled all the Bottom-60 that they can. If the movie is commercially available, then Movie Madness has it! The Bottom-60 has some nuggets too. Who's interested in seeing Brad Pitt living at BridgePort Brewery in *The Favor*? Or how about Morgan Freeman, Cate Blanchett, Burt Reynolds, Jack Black, Richard Dreyfuss, Charlize Theron, Billy Bob Thornton, Harvey Keitel, Ryan O'Neal, or Dennis Quaid...they all filmed in PDX too!

Other Filmed-in-Portland movies not on our list:

1957	Portland Expose	2006	Behind the Mask: The Rise of Leslie Vernon
1970	Five Easy Pieces (Portland scenes cut in final edit– thanks Mike for the tip)	2006	Punk Love
		2006	Old Joy
1973	Stark Raving Mad	2007	Cathedral Park
1984	Courier of Death	2007	Feast of Love**
1986	Mala Noche	2007	Mr. Brooks *not actually filmed in Portland
1986	Short Circuit		
1986	Shadowplay	2007	Music Within**
1988	Permanent Record	2007	Paranoid Park**
1989	Breaking In	2008	Management
1990	Come See the Paradise	2008	Selfless
1990	Love at Large**	2008	Twilight
1992	Dr. Giggles	2008	Wendy and Lucy
1992	Frozen Assets	2009	Assassins
1994	Imaginary Crimes	2009	Drama Queens
1994	The Favor	2009	The Burning Plain**
1995	Mr. Holland's Opus	2009	The Road
1996	Reggie's Prayer	2010	Little Blue Pill**
1997	Bongwater	2010	Extraordinary Measures**
1998	Zero Effect**	2010	Some Days are Better than Others
2000	Men of Honor		
2001	Bandits*	2011	Restless
2003	Elephant	2011	Rid of Me
2004	Graffiti Artist	2012	Blue Like Jazz
2004	What the #$*! Do We (k)πow?	2012	Cell count
2005	Bigger Than the Sky	2012	Shiver
2005	Film Geek	2013	COG
2005	Thumbsucker	2013	City Baby
2005	Damaged Goods		

**Honorable mention for pdx-Centric-ness

Dateline PDX March 1971: The world's most famous sex symbol arrives in li'l old Portland Oregon. Raquel Welch, of furry bikini *One Million Years B.C.* fame, brought her juggernaut of jiggle to North Portland and the Expo Center to shower some Hollywood star treatment to the wildly popular sport of roller derby. *Kansas City Bomber* was the first major Hollywood movie shot entirely in the Portland area and it highlighted the no-holds-barred theatrics of Roller Derby that filled the auditoriums of the day. Don't expect Shakespeare, but do expect a fun "Catfight at the EX-PO Corral" where Raquel bashes opponents with a mop, chokes an announcer and even battles her sinister teammates...all while chairs, tables, buckets and bodies fly. Adding to the roller mayhem, the shots of the rabid rink-side Portland fans are a howl, the crowd of cretins seemingly sourced from the same mental hospital that Jack Nicholson would commandeer later in *Cuckoo's Nest*.

Young Jodie Foster

The Portland scenery isn't limited to the Expo Center. Not only is there a long scene shot inside the Kenton Club (thus making it "World Famous"), you'll also see Jodie Foster as 9-year-old child in her first major-film role, roller-skating down NoPo's Fenwick St. with her mom Raquel. And, lest we forget, Raquel rocked the then-new Thunderbird Hotel with some serious va-va-voom in a '70s stretch dress that barely contained her curves. Whew, can't forget that!!

Films

PDX HIGHLIGHTS:

- Latourell Falls (The Gorge) (13:58)
- Raquel and Jodie skate on N. Fenwick St. near Bryant (15:00)
- Raquel drives over the Marquam Bridge eastbound (17:23)
- Raquel and teammate teasingly shower at the Expo Center (28:54)
- Outside the Expo Center the girls get accosted by fans (29:28)
- Raquel stays at her new friend's houseboat at Hayden Island (30:50)
- The derby crew heads to the Kenton Club, 2025 N. Kilpatrick (36:40)
- Raquel sports the semi-sheer dress on her date with Bombers' manager (47:06)
- Thunderbird Hotel at Jantzen Beach (59:51) (the hotel burned down in 2012)
- Raquel walks with her sleazy manager along the docks at Jantzen Beach just east of the I-5 Bridge (1:22:56)

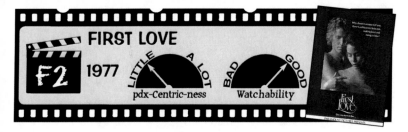

FIRST LOVE
1977
LITTLE   A LOT   BAD   GOOD
pdx-Centric-ness   Watchability
F2

First Love is a shiny diamond-in-the-rough amongst Portland's nearly-unknown historic movie catalog. What you've got here is a coming-of-age romance story filmed almost entirely on the Reed College campus. The steamy action takes place between two sexy up-and-coming young film talents, William Katt (*Greatest American Hero*) and Susan Dey (*The Partridge Family*). Copious collegiate copulation occurs before jealousy rears its ugly head and drives the wedge that...well, we won't spoil it... because the film is actually a fairly decent young-love story. For movie-goers of the day this film was a bit of a shocker because it starred teen-sensation TV-star Laurie Partridge in her first unabashedly bare-all adult "nudie" film. *People Magazine* ran a 3-page story about the eyebrows-raising movie, commenting, "The new Dey in town isn't Doris: Susan flew from TV's Partridges to a soft-core 'R'." Go ahead, carpe diem...this flick isn't a dog, and it does have its Dey.

**Mini
Pittock
Mansion**

Films

PDX HIGHLIGHTS:

- Reed College campus from the start and throughout the entire film.
- Reed Library (4:00)
- Italian Restaurant (**wow**, we have no idea...who remembers this restaurant?) (8:15)
- Reed Cafeteria (17:00)
- Stark Street Bridge over Sandy River (52:15)
- Pittock Mansion, 3229 NW Pittock Drive (52:44)
- Pittock Mansion dollhouse replica (55:44)
- Reed campus Barry Cerf Memorial Theater (1:24:55)
- Reed's old wooden stream bridge (1:26:19)
- Historic Vancouver, WA train station (now Amtrak) (1:26:45)
- Oregon Zoo (1:29:00)

UNHINGED

F3 1982

pdx-Centric-ness · Watchability

Unhinged is Portland's home-grown offering to the low-budget slasher-horror genre. Local writer/director Don Gronquist was the notable young Portland filmmaker of the day years before Gus Van Sant stole the show. For *Unhinged*, Gronquist's second film, he sourced a cast of local acting "talent" and filmed almost the entire movie up at the Pittock Mansion. Before the Pittock suspense begins though, the first minutes of the movie surprise with an introductory shower scene followed by a drive over the St. Johns Bridge and up Germantown Rd. as the three hotties head off to a weekend jazz festival.

Unhinged is actually pretty entertaining in a guilty-pleasure, low-budget, bad-acting, 80's-synthesized soundtrack sort of way. The trouble this movie had upon its release is horror-film legend, as it somehow got banned by the UK as a "Video-Nasty," along with such other truly shocking/repulsive flicks like *"I Spit on Your Grave."* This "ban" now colors peoples' expectations for the movie, making folks expect something far more gruesome, far more shocking. But *Unhinged* isn't all that "unhinged" really, by horror/slasher standards...why it ever got banned is anyone's guess. *Willamette Week* put Don Gronquist on its 8/15/12 cover and did a lengthy story about Don's entire career. In our opinion, *Unhinged* should be Portland's midnight-movie classic, much more so than *The Room*.

PDX HIGHLIGHTS:

- St. Johns Bridge (5:43)
- Germantown Rd. (note huge tree at hairpin turn) (6:12)
- Pittock Mansion bedroom, 3229 NW Pittock Dr. (10:41)
- Dialogue in the Dining Room (13:31)
- Menace in the Music Room (20:53)
- Breathing outside the bedrooms (29:25)
- Bi-Girl nude shower in the famed bathroom (32:14)
- Chopping in the woods (37:54)
- Gore in the Gift Shop (1:13:16)
- ...and then...the surprise-ending finale in the blood-spattered attic (1:15:53)

NOTE: On the DVD be sure to watch the extra 1980 Portland TV interview with young director Don!

Addendum: *Unhinged* wins out over the 1989 made-for-TV horror/thriller *The Haunting of Sarah Hardy*. *Hardy* is worth the watch for Pittock fans, as the entire thriller is set in the mansion. (P.S. *Hardy* is available for free on YouTube)

DRUGSTORE COWBOY

F4 1989

LITTLE — A LOT
pdx-Centric-ness

BAD — GOOD
Watchability

MATT DILLON ★ KELLY LYNCH

Drugstore Cowboy is hands down, the BEST PDX-centric movie ever. Hats off (the bed) to Gus. Unlike most movies on this list, this movie is both good *and* critically acclaimed—as opposed to the turds that Hollywood generally lays on Portland.

True to Van Sant form though, Gus doesn't pimp out Portland scenery too obviously in *Drugstore Cowboy*. Some good PDXccitizens with Mensa-level PDX-IQ might spot the obscure filming locations featured in this flick, but most normal folk might need help to "Cowboy-up" and become a *Drugstore* know-it-all.

Before we get all scene-ID happy, we want to give Gus a special shout-out for shooting both the opening and closing credits against the still-in-place Lovejoy Columns (Entry B4). Huzzah Gus, hooray Lovejoys, and whoop whoop for the most peculiar of PDXccentric icons living forever in Portland celluloid glory.

PDX HIGHLIGHTS:

- Lovejoy columns (Entry B4)(1:42)
- Matt Dillon Benson Bubbler, Nob Hill Pharmacy, 21st & Glisan (3:33)
- First apartment, NE 9th and Webster (8:30)
- Bob's Mom's house, N. Greenwich near Dekum (22:42)
- Josephine Apts are the Irving Condos at 2127 NW Irving St (25:02)
- Panda runs south on 13th between Glisan and Flanders (26:58)
- Panda leads cops back to Bob and Diane's apartment at NW Marshall near 26th across from Chapman School (27:18)
- Second heist, SE Belmont at 60th, the old Seaton Pharmacy (42:22)
- Union Ave. Motel is still at 59 NE Gertz Rd. The room featured is the first stand-alone room east of the office and it still has the same red curtains (44:02)
- Emmanuel Hospital (49:25)
- St. Francis Hotel was at SW 11th and Main St. The hotel fell to the wrecking ball in 2001 (1:10:17)

Films

MY OWN PRIVATE IDAHO

F5 1991

pdx-Centric-ness — LITTLE / A LOT

Watchability — BAD / GOOD

MOPI is a strange film, no denying that. Gus Van Sant's third film is three different movie ideas morphed into one. *MOPI*, taking its name from a B-52's song, is a bit song-like with its vague and wandering "plot," as opposed to the structured narrative story portrayed in *Drugstore Cowboy*. *MOPI* seems surreal and dream-like as the bi-sexual street hustlers River Phoenix and Keanu Reeves prowl and carouse the streets of Portland. *Idaho*, like *Drugstore*, features a "dark" Portland chock-full-o' the seedier side of the city.

People either love *My Own Private Idaho* or hate it. Truth be told, we used to hate it, but now we love it. It was a success with the critics and is considered a PDX classic just like its famed brother *Drugstore Cowboy*.

PDX HIGHLIGHTS:

- Opening scene road, near Maupin on Hwy 216. Coords:45.260974 -120.978297 (0:50) (49:30) (1:10:00)
- Farmhouse, The Dalles: 45.541704 -121.024302 (16:30) (1:27:00)
- Video Follies adult bookstore, no longer there, 915 SW 3rd (17:34)
- Thompson Elk Statue with a painted Indian atop it and stealing the name *Coming of the White Man* from Washington Park's statue (21:19)
- Lamthong Restaurant (Bailey's Taproom) 213 SW Broadway (22:00)
- Atop the Governor Hotel, transposed with views from parking garage across from Lotus Bar/Lownsdale Sq. Bob emerges where I-84 meets I-5 (27:00)
- Inside the Governor Hotel, now Jakes Grill (28:30)
- Cathedral Park and St. Johns Bridge (Entry D4) (34:41)
- Motorcycling down SW Broadway at Oak past Mary's Club (38:14)
- Exterior of the derelict Governor Hotel (bashing door of Jake's Grill) (44:21)
- Thunderbird Hotel Jantzen Beach (burned 2012) Gus cameo (1:04:30)
- Across the street from Weinhard's Brewery, Burnside and 11th (1:26:30)
- Great NW Books (now American Apparel), Stark and Burnside (1:27:50)
- Jake's Famous Crawfish exterior scenes (1:28:44)
- Huber's interior restaurant (1:29:01)
- Riverview Cemetery, battling funerals (1:34:00)

Films

BODY OF EVIDENCE

F6 1993

pdx-Centric-ness — LITTLE / A LOT

Watchability — BAD / GOOD

Madonna, fresh off the release of her show-all coffee-table *SEX* book, riles-up "small town" (her words) Portland in this critically-slammed erotic courtroom thriller. Strangely enough, before the movie began shooting around the city, Madonna was gifted a key to the city in a ceremony crafted by Commissioner Lindberg. The 4-foot-tall "key" was adorned with a tacky garter belt and lace stocking. Hilariously, Madonna refused to even touch the thing during the televised presentation (YouTube on our website).

The critics jumped all over *Body of Evidence* for both its turgid courtroom action (filmed in the Washington State Capitol Building in Olympia) and its over-the-top sexual shenanigans. But, the way we see it here at Xccentral, when the movie isn't confusing you with its courtroom showdown, the out-of-court action is literally quite titillating, and the Portland scenery quite recognizable.

The Oregonian/BRENT WOJAHN

Portland Commissioner Mike Lindberg (right) gives a garter-belted key to the city to Madonna, her press agent Liz Rosenberg, and co-star Willem Dafoe during a news conference Sunday at the Benson Hotel.

Oregonian 4-6-1992

Films

PDX HIGHLIGHTS:

- Pittock Mansion, Madonna sexes a man to death (First 4 minutes)
- Burial scene stars the Lone Fir Cemetery, SE 26th & Stark (4:16)
- Unknown restaurant **(Help...where is this???)** (7:00)
- Portlandia statue makes its controversial Hollywood debut in a brief walk-under cameo shot (App 6)(8:31)
- U.S. Customs House, 220 NW 8th (12:07)
- Acupuncture scene shot in building across the street from Darcelle's, at 3rd and Davis (18:08)
- Sellwood dock houseboat (featuring one of the houseboats which is normally moored near Oaks Park) (21:36), (36:00), (67:00), and finale

FREE WILLY

F7 1993

pdx-Centric-ness — LITTLE / A LOT

Watchability — BAD / GOOD

FREE WILLY

Free Willy is ostensibly about a boy and a killer whale, but through our Xccentric-colored glasses we see a movie starring Portland and Astoria. Right from the movie's start, after a few minutes dickering around catching Willy, the PDXploits begin with a nefarious youth gang of homeless pre-teens who spend their days panhandling at Pioneer Courthouse Square and eating behind the Burnside skate park. Running afoul of the law the charming young miscreant Jesse leads the police on a chase through downtown PDX before sneaking into Oaks Amusement Park to continue his crime spree. Jesse gets busted, but not before befriending a whale. *Free Willy* then translocates Oaks Park and Keiko's real-life Mexican water park to the Oregon Coast… where everything gets adorably sappy until the happy ending.

PDX HIGHLIGHTS:

- Panhandling at Pioneer Courthouse Square (5:17).
- Loco's Restaurant—the IHOP at SW Park Ave, no longer there (6:00).
- Hijinks under the Burnside Bridge while the skaters ride the not-quite-finished Burnside skate park (7:00).
- Gang flees under the Morrison Bridge only to pop up surface-side at the waterfront steps beside the Salmon Street Springs Fountain, Hawthorne Bridge in the rear (8:00).
- Oaks Amusement Park (10:40)(17:25)(35:57)
- Jesse's foster parents house, 34th and Harrison in Astoria (13:30)
- Oaks Park house (Randall's house) that overhangs the Willamette (18:55) (33:00) (48:29)
- Jesse rides his bike across the Hawthorne Bridge (35:56) (53:13)
- After leaving the 14th Street dock in Astoria Jesse rides his bike back via the Hawthorne Bridge (52:13)
- The shop where Jesse's foster dad works, 5931 SE 52nd Ave Portland (54:58) (1:28:08)
- Ecola State Park Oregon Coast (1:13:27)
- Jesse and the gang decide to free Willy so fake-o-Keiko takes a ride on a flatbed across the Hawthorne (1:29:16).
- Splash and Dash car wash, 7111 NE MLK Jr. Drive (1:35:59)
- The Marina where Willy is released is Hammond Mooring Basin in Hammond, OR (just NW of Astoria) (1:37:13)

Films

THE TEMP
1993

pdx-Centric-ness · LITTLE — A LOT

Watchability · BAD — GOOD

F8

The Temp is an impossibly implausible corporate "thriller" where Timothy Hutton plays an up-and-coming cookie company executive, Faye Dunaway plays his boss, and the vampy Lara Flynn Boyle is hired as his temp. This movie is bizarre, but its odd twists, turns, gore, and deaths keep the laughable action moving along nicely. As the cookie begins to crumble and it seems that the chips are down for Appleby Cookie Co., Lara Flynn Boyle takes matters into her own hands and the body count rises…and… well, we won't spoil the fun nonsense for you (the original ending of the movie tested sooo bad that the studio had to graft-on a new ending, but to no avail, as it still sucks. We have an *LA Times* article about it on our website.) Critics pummeled this movie for good reason, the *Washington Post* calling it a "semi-comic thriller" featuring a baffled cast. Regardless of the ridiculousness, the recognizable big-budget Portland action is non-stop…making *The Temp* an Xccentric guilty pleasure.

Timothy Hutton and Lara Flynn Boyle stroll the park blocks

PDX HIGHLIGHTS:

- Sentinel (ex-Governor) Hotel as Appleby HQ, 11th and Alder (1:46)
- The Sellwood Bridge from Portland Yacht Club (12:31)
- The cookie execs attend a Blazers game at the Rose Garden (14:56)
- Marquam bridge mayhem (33:00)
- Inside/outside Kells, 112 SW 2nd (37:00)
- South Park Blocks (43:40)
- Battleground Lake skinny-dip, 18002 NE 249th, Battleground, WA (50:40)
- Basketball under Morrison Bridge Tom McCall Waterfront Park (59:?0)
- Bar fight scene (**we have no idea…help!**) (1:14:16)
- Oregon Coast Hwy at Neahkanie Mtn, Manzanita (1:20:00)

Films

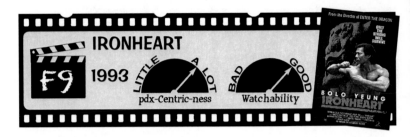

IRONHEART
1993

pdx-Centric-ness · Watchability

Ironheart is the best kung-fu movie <u>ever</u> made in Portland, being the <u>only</u> kung-fu movie made in Portland. But understand this, Grasshopper, this movie isn't the best because it's good—nope, it's because it's horribly bad, stars the classic kung-fu villain Bolo Yeung, and it features classic 1990 Portland footage that makes us high-five in PDXccentric joy. 'Nuff said?

Ironheart, though virtually unknown to Portlanders, is actually a medium-budget chop-socky directed by none other than, whoa, the director of *Enter The Dragon*. The movie was filmed all over the Portland area

and the 1990 scenery is sweet—you'll see the White Stag sign, *Portlandia* statue and Portland Building, a bubbler…and, neatest of neat… under the Burnside Bridge just months before the skate rogues began constructing the now-famed Burnside skate park (E3). Oh my!

All balanced critique aside, this is one of our favorite-ever PDX movies. Never heard of it? Don't feel alone, as few people even know *Ironheart* exists. *Ironheart* is, in essence, what this PDX book is about—the hidden gems of Portland that exist in secrecy, waiting to be re-discovered.

Rally yourself, watch *Ironheart* and you'll be glad you did.

Sorry, but only available on VHS. Read a hilarious review on MonsterHunterMovieReviews.com.

PDX HIGHLIGHTS:

- Club Upfront FX (now closed). Near Mill Ends at 823 SW Naito (:30)
- Port of Portland (6:00)
- The Skyline Tavern, 8031 NW Skyline Blvd (13:46)
- Fight scene on beach, west side of BNSF RR bridge, 45.580732 -122.744840 (16:07)
- The Portland Oregon sign in the era of "White Stag" (20:19)
- Portlandia statue (used without permission) 1120 SW 5th (20:52)
- Washington Park steps above amphitheater (23:10)
- The Greenwood Inn (demolished 2006), 10700 SW Allen Blvd Beaverton (27:00)
- Milverstead HQ across from City Hall, star Britton Lee drinks from a Benson Bubbler, 1211 SW 5th (33:00)
- Ankeny Square (and for PDX nerds, the old Francis J. Murnane dock just south of the Burnside Bridge) SW Naito and Ankeny (34:40)
- Car chase ends under the Burnside Bridge only months before skaters started work on the Burnside skate park (E3) (45:08) (59:10)
- Waverly Yacht Club, 513 SE Marion St Sellwood (47:50) (52:50)
- Milverstead HQ battle, 1211 SW 5th and Jefferson (1:01:50)
- Port of Portland finale (1:14:00)

Films

HEAR NO EVIL

F10 1993

LITTLE · A LOT
pdx-Centric-ness

BAD · GOOD
Watchability

Hear No Evil is a bad movie, but it's a fun-to-watch bad movie filmed almost entirely in PDX with tons of recognizable Portland scenery. What bits of the movie that aren't filmed in PDX are filmed in the oh-so-recognizable Columbia River Gorge and, even more amazingly, the most filming ever done inside and around Timberline Lodge!

Hear No Evil, like *The Temp*, was filmed big-budget style with big stars. Regrettably, also similar to *The Temp*, *Hear No Evil* turned out to be such a bad movie that the studio had to re-jig the ending and even change the name of the movie from its original title "Danger Sign." We could go on and on about this movie's delightful awfulness, but we think the *NY Times* summed it up fairly well with their 1993 review: "Although the film has serviceable performances, they cannot cover up the story's gaping holes or the thudding predictability of the screenplay…. With gobs of pretty scenery, it is, if nothing else, an effective travel brochure for the Pacific Northwest."

Explosion on the Hawthorne Bridge!

PDX HIGHLIGHTS:

- Lewis & Clark College, Frank Manor House, 615 SW Palatine Hill Rd. (:30)
- Westside waterfront (3:20)
- Unknown park scene **(help us!)** (4:21)
- Marlee's SW Market St. apartment building (12:45) multiple
- Under the Broadway Bridge (15:00)
- Key Largo club (Whiskey Bar), 31 NW 1st Ave. (17:20)
- Union Station (17:50)
- Salmon Street Springs fountain and Naito Pkwy (A9) (19:38)
- Hawthorne Bridge WOW!! (20:10) (*Oregonian* article on our website)
- Washington Park Rose Test Garden (21:45)
- On the night skyline you can see the Portland Oregon Sign when it still read "White Stag"—look quick (B15) (48:52)
- Octagon house-on-a-pedestal, SW Fairmount St. (54:30) (59:00)
- Washington Park reservoir (1:04:09)
- Houseboat near Oaks Park, 6901 SE Oaks Pkwy (1:05:40)
- Timberline Lodge (1:13:35) (1:17:30-to-end)
- Columbia Gorge "The Hatchery" windsurf launch (1:14:20)

Films

BRAINSMASHER: A LOVE STORY

F11 1993

pdx-Centric-ness — LITTLE / A LOT

Watchability — BAD / GOOD

Brainsmasher features an Academy Award winning Andrew Dice Clay as a professor at Reed who meets bookish genius Teri Hatcher at a clandestine Mensa meet-up and together they conjoin their Hi-IQ capabilities to unravel…oh, oops…wrong movie…sorry.

In reality, *Brainsmasher* is an Andrew Dice Clay vehicle filmed as an action-movie send-up—a so-called "action comedy." Dice, not long before his career completely crapped-out, plays a tough guy bouncer. Teri Hatcher joins him as a supermodel-on-a-mission. Together they mock 1980s action movies during a breathless one-night romp throughout downtown Portland.

As dicey as this movie is, it's actually ~~fun~~ ok to watch as long as you know that it was filmed as a mockery—if it were trying to be good then it'd be dumbingly awful. Like Nigel said in *Spinal Tap*, "It's such a fine line between stupid, an uh, clever."

Don't expect a good movie, but give Dice a roll and the payoff will be lots of spoof gags and a whole lotta early-'90s downtown Portland. If you knew early-'90s downtown Portland really well, this movie will give you some neat flashback moments, as well as the longest scene ever filmed inside Mary's Club.

PDX HIGHLIGHTS:

(All times taken from Netflix streaming version of movie)
- Warehouse, 608 NW 13th St at Hoyt (4:15) (1:07:00)
- China Gate, NW 4th and Burnside (9:45)
- Fence jump, 769 SW Ankeny at 8th (11:30)
- Asian Restaurant corner, SW Broadway and Ankeny (11:53)
- Zebra Club, 722 SW Taylor and Broadway (12:05)
- Hop on the Max from Galleria skywalk, SW 10th and Morrison (19:30)
- Old Music Box and Fox Theaters glimpse (now Fox Tower), SW Broadway and Yamhill (24:10)
- Pioneer Courthouse Square walk-through (25:20)
- Thru Lownsdale Square to Lotus Hotel, SW 3rd and Salmon (30:50)
- Police Station building **(HELP!)** (41:24) (49:11)
- Abercrombie & Fitch corner, Teri in window poster, SW Morrison and Broadway (49:25)
- Teri walks around corner from Salmon onto SW 9th, walking by the old B. Moloch's with the original Widmer sign above (entry A2) (51:18)
- Guild Theater, 829 SW 9th (53:40) (1:03:35)
- Inside Mary's Club fight scene, 129 SW Broadway (53:50)
- St Patrick's Church, 1635 NW 19th and Savier (1:05:25)
- Dance Club finale (help!?)(1:10:40)

Films

FOXFIRE 1996

LITTLE — A LOT
pdx-Centric-ness

BAD — GOOD
Watchability

Amongst the pantheon of Portland-made movies on this list, *Foxfire* should be better-known. *Foxfire*, while winning no awards for either plot or acting, wins huge plaudits for its iconic Portland filming locations and its cast of surprising young actresses/actors.

In a nutshell, the unheralded 21-year-old Angelina Jolie storms into Portland and proceeds to make a one-woman raid on Lincoln High School where she adopts a gang of misfit girls. Her grrrl gang, faced with a variety of social injustices, turns to a life of crime and quasi-lesbianism to right their wrongs.

The acting surprises begin from the get-go. The movie's first scene features the female co-star snapping pix of her very naked boyfriend in the woods. This dashing and unabashed fellow became a whole lot more famous a dozen years later when he appeared in a box-office smash...as...Dr. Carlisle Cullen! The next surprise is young Angelina herself, starring in this film with her then girlfriend Jenny Shimizu. Angie's list of surprises doesn't stop, as she soon had most of her gang out of their shirts and getting their boobs tattooed with a foxfire glyph. Another of the grrrl gang, Jenny Lewis, had her sights on a rock 'n' roll future, becoming the leader of the indie-band Rilo Kiley. The fifth grrrl, Sarah Rosenberg, turned out to be a local gal who for a time worked for Mike Clark at Movie Madness. Who Knew??!!

Broadway Bridge, Vista suicide bridge, Lovejoy Columns, Burnside skate park, the slammer....crime spree mayhem...*Foxfire* HELL YEAH!!!!

PDX HIGHLIGHTS:

- Naked in the woods: Dr. Carlisle Cullen! (opening scene)
- Lincoln High, 1600 SW Salmon (2:07 assault) (24:19 principal's office) (30:53 sprinklers)
- Vista Viaduct Bridge, 1267 SW Vista (19:49) (underneath 44:50) (selfie 58:45) (boy trouble 1:06:00)
- Broadway Bridge (climbs 20:10) (girls prance 58:22)(finale 1:32:36)
- Mystery House in woods **(help!)** (27:45)
- Burnside Skatepark, 35 NE 2nd (57:35)
- Tai-chi window, SW 14th and Washington (58:03)
- Walk-thru field w/bus NW 19th and Madison (58:30)
- North Park Blocks, NW 9th and Davis (59:00)
- Chase scene from SW Corbett Ave to SW Nebraska to SW Macadam (round and round as they pass the same building 3 times) (1:07:40)
- Car tumbles down hill off NW Westover Terrace Rd where the Westover Condos are now, NW 24th and Glisan (1:09:48)
- Lovejoy Columns, OG spot, NW Lovejoy and 12th (1:12:37) (1:17:35)
- Col. River Correctional Inst. 9111 NE Sunderland (1:13:40) (1:19:25)

TOTAL REALITY

F13 1997

pdx-Centric-ness: LITTLE — A LOT

Watchability: BAD — GOOD

Star Wars meets *Terminator* (well, not really) in this big medium-budget Sci-Fi flick. *Total Reality* is Portland's only appearance in a "major" Sci-Fi movie and that alone makes this movie watchable, at least for a Portlander. The plot is a bit muddy, but it has something to do with soldiers from a blighted future returning to 1998 Portland to alter the past and

Skidmore Fountain

thus change the future from bad to good. And hey, just like the possible future that may possibly happen if the time-troops complete this mission impossible, this movie's plot also veers drunkenly from bad to good. Good are the *Star Wars*-esque extravagant space scenes, bad are the earthly shoot-outs…good are the numerous HUGE explosions around PDX, bad

Shoot-out on the Hawthorne Bridge

are the costumes, dialog, characters and plot. Good are the iconic PDX scene locations like the Skidmore Fountain and the climactic shoot-out mayhem on the Hawthorne Bridge. We say two thumbs up for eccentric Portlanders, two thumbs down for the rest of the galaxy.

Films

PDX HIGHLIGHTS:

- Montgomery Park atrium, 2701 NW Vaughn (2:34) (59:52)
- Unknown Bridges house explosion **(help!)** (33:00**)**
- Unknown house car explosion **(help!)** (40:00)
- Pool hall shootout, 126 SW 2nd St (next to Kells)(49:00), (then at 1:08:20 as Cyber Café)
- Oregon City industrial snippets (58:38)
- Train tracks scene **(help!??!)**…(58:52)
- Ankeny Square Skidmore Fountain (1:07:16)
- Hawthorne Bridge shoot-out and explosion (1:12:07)
- Hawthorne Bridge splashes (1:14:07)
- Eastbank Esplanade Portland Fire Dept bldg (rebuilt 2014) (1:16:17)

DOWN & OUT WITH THE DOLLS

F14 2001

LITTLE · A LOT
pdx-Centric-ness

BAD · GOOD
Watchability

Down and Out with the Dolls is a rollicking indie flick about an all-g*rrrl* rock band trying to make it big in circa 2000-ish Portland. While no movie is ever going to really nail the Portland rock scene, *D&O w/D* does a fun job of capturing the chaotic vibe. Don't expect Shakespearean acting from the actual rocker chicks who play the Paper Dolls, but do expect an entertaining Portland-riffic traipse throughout recognizable PDX via bikes, skateboards and beater vans as the Dolls rock-out at backyard parties and even a big show at the Satyricon.

For us minutiae-seeking authors, we had fun gasps of surprise identifying odd little PDXccentric spots throughout the movie. Besides the innards of both the famed Satyricon and Fellini...get ready to pause the remote for glimpses of Share-It Square, Burnside Skatepark, Hung Far Low, and even Paul Bunyan making his big screen debut. Yowsa!

PDX HIGHLIGHTS:

- Share-It Square (App 3, #27) (2:02) & (1:16:28)
- Fellini Restaurant (now closed and demolished) 125 NW 6th (3:36)
- Salmon Street Springs Fountain (A9) (11:11)
- Yamhill Max Station (11:12)
- Vita Café (original café across from current) 3023 NE Alberta (11:14)
- Biking across the Broadway Bridge (14:56)
- Portland Storage Company, 215 SE Morrison (15:07)
- Burnside Skatepark (E3) (25:56)
- Washougal River Dougan Falls (29:10)
- Made in Oregon Sign (B15) (32:02)
- Satyricon Club (now closed and demolished) 125 NW 6th (32:08)
- Original Hung Far Low entrance awning (B12) (52:47)
- China Gate, Burnside and 4th (52:53)
- Irvington Park (53:21)
- Fight in parking lot of Portland Yacht Club (1:17:05)
- Kenton's Paul Bunyan (D8) (1:22:41)

Films

THE HUNTED

F15 2003

LITTLE — A LOT
pdx-Centric-ness

BAD — GOOD
Watchability

The Hunted is the oft-maligned action-thriller filmed almost entirely in Portland. Tommy Lee Jones and Benicio Del Toro star in this *First Blood*-esque war veteran-gone-crazy chase-'em-up.

For the first hour of *The Hunted* Portland only shows up in short and unsatisfying snippets. But, at minute 65 the PDX action begins to boil-over when Benicio Del Rambo pokes his head out of a manhole and then, WHOA, the next 15 minutes

Portland's own "Mr. Statue"

are a tour-de-force translocational romp through downtown Portland. Then, after Benicio hucks off a downtown bridge and somehow reappears at Willamette Falls, the movie stealthily moves the final climactic knife fight to Washington's now-removed Elwha Dam.

PDX HIGHLIGHTS:

- Gus J. Solomon Courthouse, 620 SW Main (32:37)
- Cornell Road tunnel, 3052 NW Cornell (42:49)
- Jeff Gianola (KOIN TV) at the Cornell tunnel (49:25)
- Benicio's girlfriend's house, NE 8th near Failing. (50:17)
- South Park Blocks and back side of the Shnitz (59:13)
- Manhole Benicio pop-up, Broadway and Stark (1:05:13)
- Benson Bubbler/Dekum Bldg, SW 3rd and Washington (1:06:00)
- Terry Schrunk Park, 4th and Madison (1:06:54)
- Burnside Skatepark cameo, 33 NE 2nd (1:07:18)
- Keller Fountain, 4th and Clay (1:07:30)
- Steel Bridge off ramp wall (NW 3rd and Glisan St) (1:08:30)
- Tom McCall waterfront, biking under Hawthorne and past a cameo of PDX busker Mr. Statue (Silver man, painted white) (1:09:18)
- Hawthorne Bridge action begins with two buses connected to emulate a MAX train (1:09:54)
- Benicio climbs bridge and jumps into the Willamette (1:13:22)
- Ross Island Beach, Ross Island Bridge views (1:14:30)
- Willamette Falls and power plant ruins, Benicio crafts a knife, 276 Tumwater Dr. (in river) Oregon City (1:14:50)
- Elwha Dam Wash. final knife fight (dam removed 2012) (1:20:30)

SPIRAL
F16 2007
LITTLE — A LOT
pdx-Centric-ness
BAD — GOOD
Watchability
SPIRAL

Spiral is a suspenseful thriller of the geek-gone-bad ilk that showcases an impressive PDX-centric lineup of recognizable locations. The movie is good enough to keep you gripped with its drama despite the lead actor's weak-chin'd snivelings.

Wapato

Weak chin or not though, director/star Joel David Moore not only co-starred in the world's highest grossing movie, *Avatar*...but also has a Mattel action figure crafted in his likeness, whoa.

Under the direction of local-boy Moore, *Spiral* celebrates the Portland skyline with lingering panoramas...while our bridges, parks, cemetery,

Laurelhurst

and never-opened prison (D1) get fondled nicely too. Overall, the movie isn't a tight spiral, but for Portlanders it's worth a watch. Yay Mt. Tabor, yay Laurelhurst!

Films

PDX HIGHLIGHTS:

- Fullers Café, 136 NW 9th (:40) (9:19)
- Telemarketing Office, Wapato Jail, 14355 N Bybee Lake Ct (2:59) (multiple scenes)
- Mt. Tabor basketball courts, SE Salmon Way (18:17) (53:00)
- Crossroads Music on 3130 SE Hawthorne Blvd (36:01)
- Laurelhurst Park duck pond, SE Oak and Cesar Chavez (37:17)
- Walking past Yoga in the Pearl and Yoshida, NW 9th and Davis (41.29)
- Clinton Street Theater (walking past Café Broder, Savoy Tavern, Clinton St Records), 2522 SE Clinton (47:17)
- Lone Fir Cemetery, SE Stark and SE 26th (51:47)

THE AUTEUR

F17 2008 pdx-Centric-ness Watchability

Watch this movie! *The Auteur* is Portland as fuck, literally. Local filmmaker James Westby begins the movie with sweeping PDX vistas and then dives in using local actors for this uproarious mockumentary about an aging porn director who arrives in Portland for a career retrospective show at the Clinton Theater. This little-known flick is hilarious, PDX-centric, and as unabashedly in-your-face naked as a movie can be without being X-rated. The gratuitous nudity, often featuring famed PDX strippers like Viva Las Vegas and Malice 666, is mostly comedic-type nudity rather than erotic sexuality.

The Auteur lampoons both the porn industry and Hollywood "auteur" directors such as Stanley Kubrick...and Westby totally nails it, injecting wonderfully funny subtleties at every chance. Arturo Domingo, the lead character and so-called "Kubrick of porn" not only resembles Kubrick, but he also plays chess on the set with his star just like Kubrick famously did with George C. Scott on the set of Dr. Strangelove. And then, in the clever parody of *Five Easy Pieces* titled, *Five Easy Nieces*, actor Breen mimics Jack Nicholson's piano-prodigy character by banging on a piano while he bangs upon one of the nieces—a hilarious touch! Also, the mocking porn titles are laugh-out-loud classic; *Children of a Lesser Wad, All That Jizz, Purple Vein, Broadway Danny's Hos*, etc. Bravo James Westby!

It's hard for us to believe that we had watched over 50 Portland-centric

  films before *The Auteur* came to our attention. *The Auteur* is a Portland underground classic and nearly as fun as the annual World Naked Bike Ride.

PDX HIGHLIGHTS:

- Portland highways and bridges intro
- Jupiter Hotel, 800 E Burnside (5:00) (31:20) (1:06:30)
- SW Broadway at Ankeny (Danny and the Hos) (11:10)
- Sauvie Island Collins Beach, 38149 NW Reeder Rd (14:11) (1:01:30, with (D2) UFO-boat in distance)
- Clinton St. Theater, 2522 SE Clinton (18:33) (42:00, w/Ron Jeremy) (1:01:20)
- TV "Let's Get Fucked" film patio Irving Street Lofts, 1314 NW Irving St (43:00) (Thank you John Breen)
- VideoRama, 2640 NE Alberta (56:10)
- East side intersection/cops scene, 9th and SE Yamhill (59:00)

Films

UNTRACEABLE

F18 2008

pdx-Centric-ness | Watchability

Untraceable is a horror thriller pitting a cyber-wizard killer against the Portland Police and FBI Cyber-crimes unit. Diane Lane plays a tough-as-megapixels FBI agent who stumbles upon a website called "killwithme.com" where an ingeniously "untraceable" cyber terrorist tortures to death an assortment of everyday people. The psycho's killer-app is that the torture become more severe when more people log onto his website to watch the creative gruesomeness. Whew, this is not a flick for the squeamish! Diane super-sleuths the hidden pattern to the killings, and the feverish manhunt accelerates, but, alas, not before the torture-spree strikes close to home... then *even closer* to home.

Portland scenery is abundant throughout all the horrifying and suspenseful edge-of-your-seat action, especially beaucoup Broadway Bridge

BROADWAY BRIDGE STANDOFF FOX

and other Hollywood faves such as Burnside Skatepark. Overall, *Untraceable* is one of Portland's best suspense thrillers, definitely bettering *The Hunted*, *Hear No Evil* and *Body of Evidence*.

PDX HIGHLIGHTS:

- Broadway Bridge (9:35)
- Traffic jam on ramp onto I-84 from I-5 (9:48)
- Accident on N. Mississippi under the I-405 interchange (10:26)
- Diane Lane's house, NE 18th and Tillamook (10:43) (53:30)
- Rose Garden parking lot (Moda Center) (16:15)
- Portland Rowing Club houseboats (20:38)
- Portland City Hall (29:17)
- Decoy house false alarm, NE 18th and Prescott (30:10)
- Oaks Park Roller Rink birthday party (35:22)
- Burnside Skatepark (41:20)
- False alarm house, SE Carlton near 39th (46:58)
- Diane's motel, Park Lane Inn, SW King & Yamhill (1:07:52) (1:19:37)
- Broadway Bridge suicide helicopter news footage (1:13:22)
- Fake diner in parking lot under the Broadway Bridge (1:13:40)
- Killer's house, NE 24th and Wasco (1:15:01)
- Broadway Bridge car trouble for Diane, with Albers mural (1:21:25)

Films

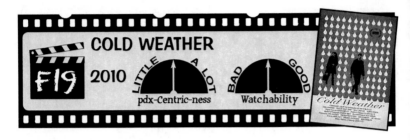

COLD WEATHER
F19 2010

LITTLE · A LOT
pdx-Centric-ness

BAD · GOOD
Watchability

Cold Weather

Cold Weather is a leisurely-paced indie flick that just feels Portlandish. What the hell does "Portlandish" mean anyways?

Expect lingering indie-ness. *Cold Weather* is about people, about how peoples' jobs don't necessarily define their lives, about how peoples' lives might not be what they seem on the surface. The *Cold Weather* plot is drizzly to begin with, but be patient and halfway through the pace quickens as so-and-so gets (???) and then is discovered to be a (???), but in trouble because (???). Whoa, a whodunnit breaks out and the Portland slackers are on the case! Round and round Portland we go, and hahaha, where this movie stops (literally)…no one knows.

Us Xccentrix like *Cold Weather*, in an uber-PDX kind of way, as did *Oregonian* reviewer Shawn Levy who wrote, "A delicately moody Sherlockian Portland hipster mystery…This son of Portland (Katz) has crafted a clouds-and-all portrait of home that feels more like my town than just about anything I've ever seen—a harder trick than it would seem."

Whoa, high praise indeed. Maybe a movie showing regular Portlanders doing regular Portland stuff like reading *Sherlock Holmes*, solving mysteries, posing for nudie mags, and foiling the baddies…well, maybe that's what everyone wants—just to see Portlanders act like Portlanders. Who needs work…we've better things to do! Best watched on a drizzly winter day with an IBU above 70.

PDX HIGHLIGHTS:

- Apartment Bldg, 31st & Burnside (1:40) (34:00 grapes) (56:58)
- Broder Café, 2508 SE Clinton (14:30)
- The Dalles, Gem Ice, 3003 E 2nd St (9:30)
- Multnomah Falls (20:40)
- Quick Bagdad Theater, 3702 SE Hawthorne (27:04)
- Skyline Restaurant, 1313 NW Skyline (27:19) (43:30)
- PSU Library,1875 SW Park Ave (51:15) (59:41)
- Broadway Cigar, 3613 NE Broadway (54.51)
- Hollywood Grocery Outlet, 4420 NE Hancock (58:50)
- Footbridge, SE 16th and Brooklyn (removed in 2014) (1:01:56)
- Washington Park amphitheater (1:04:45)
- Apartments at NE 26th and Glisan (1:10:40)
- Pambiche Restaurant glimpse, NE 28th & Glisan (1:18:25)
- U-Store Self-Storage, 1130 NE 28th (1:20:00)
- Le Bistro Montage, 301 SE Morrison (1:23:53)
- Rooftop of parking garage, SW 4th and Ash (1:32:05)

GONE
F20 2012
pdx-Centric-ness · Watchability
LITTLE — A LOT · BAD — GOOD

Gone has a hole in its plot about 15 feet deep. Usually a plot with holes would be bad, but maybe not this time. Maybe.

This suspenseful thriller features wide-eyed Amanda Seyfried as a violent femme who's hopping mad that her sister is "gone sister gone" and has been stuffed down a deep hole in Forest Park. The police don't believe Amanda, so she takes matters into her own hands and plays cat and mouse with the police all over Portland. Amanda races against time to save her sister, while she also tries to outrun all the faults in this movie's plot. On the whole this flick is fast-paced and watchable as it lavishes attention on Portland's beautiful skyline, greenery, and bridges...but alas, the critics hated it because the plot suffers more than just one hole.

Seyfried trying to outrun the bad plot

PDX HIGHLIGHTS:

- Forest Park (opening scenes)
- The gym is the Yale Union Laundry Building at SE 10th and Morrison (also Bella's ballet studio in *Twilight*) (7:49)
- Burnside Bridge looking at Big Pink and the Portland sign (8:34)
- Amanda's café job is at Genie's Cafe, 1101 SE Division (10:44)
- Downtown Self-Storage, 13th and Johnson (13:00)
- Police station is US Customs House, NW 8th and Everett (16:40)
- Locksmith is in back of Yale Union Laundry building (30:52)
- W.C. Wink Hardware, SE 2nd and Stark (40:51)
- South Park Blocks at Columbia Street (41:14)
- Ladd's Addition Circle at Harrison Ave. (47:43)
- Hotel is the building the Montage shares, 728 SE 3rd (51:24)
- Car chase under Morrison Bridge ramps (1:02:20)
- Crossing the St. Johns Bridge (1:08:50)
- Abductor tells Amanda on phone a true-life Forest Park story (1:14:30)

Films

APPENDIX 1
Hot, Not, or Learn-a-Lot

1. **Venus de Arles** Montgomery Park atrium: 2701 NW Vaughn St.

2. **Sacajawea and Jean-Baptiste** by Alice Cooper: Washington Park.

3. **Joy** by Frederic Littman: Council Crest.

4. **Skidmore Fountain** by Olin Levi Warner: SW 1st and Ankeny St.

5. **Kvinneakt** by Norman J. Taylor: SW 6th and Morrison.

6. **Pioneer Courthouse Caryatids**: 700 SW 6th Ave.

7. **Quest** by Count Alexander Von Svoboda: 900 SW 5th Ave.

8. **Portlandia** by Raymond Kaskey: 1120 SW 5th Ave.

9. **The Shemanski Fountain's Rebecca at the Well** (statue) by Oliver Laurence Barrett: SW Park and Salmon.

10. **Mistral #2** by Frederic Littman: 1219 SW Park Ave.

11. **Farewell to Orpheus** by Frederic Littman: SW Park and Mill St.

12. **The Dreamer** by Manuel Izquerdo: Pettgrove Park SW 2nd Ave.

13. **Vera Katz** by Bill Bane: Eastbank Esplanade under the Hawthorne Bridge

14. **The Dream** by Michael F. Dente: NE MLK Blvd and Holladay.

15. **Ideals** by Muriel Castanis: 800 NE Oregon St.

16. **A Neighborhood Gardener** by Tad Savinar: Holladay Park NE 11th and Multnomah.

17. **Joan of Arc** by Emmanuel Frémiet: Coe Circle NE Cesar Chavez Blvd and Glisan.

Hot, Not, or Learn-a-Lot is meant to be a playful and informative tour of Portland's female statuary. Since Facebook basically started as a "Hot or Not" contest we figured that if it worked for them, then why not us? The female statues around PDX have fun and interesting stories to tell—much more so than their male counterparts (possibly reflecting life itself). Mini-Portlandias? World-famed flasher? The largest chunk of marble? Caryatids of both wood and bronze? A babe's arm holding an apple?

Go forth and learn...go forth and judge...go forth to gaze upon Portland's statuesque females!

1. Venus de Arles: *Arles* is a replica statue that graces the very top of the elevator column inside Montgomery Park's immense glass atrium. It's difficult to see *Arles* way up there, so be sure to bring a zoom camera. Because she's so far away and hard to see, we could easily just leave her out of this Hot/Not listing...but *Arles* actually helps define why we call this

appendix Hot, Not, or Learn a Lot. The topless *Arles* might be hot or not...but far more fun, at least to us, is how much there is to learn about concerning this statue.

However, Aimee implores me not to describe in lengthy detail everything I learn about, so at her behest I'll try to be brief here, while also hoping to whet your curiosity. First, *Arles*, just like her cousin *Venus de Milo*, was found without arms. But, *Arles* was "restored" soon after her discovery, adding the arms holding both apple and mirror. *Venus de Milo* would have held the same items when she was whole, but after the Louvre obtained her they purposely obfuscated her origins for their own aggrandizement...and somewhere along her road to international fame her apple was lost. Second, the apple and mirror are <u>important</u>, as they are the beginning of a fabulous story that ends with the famous Trojan Horse. *Arles'* apple is none other than the "Apple of Discord" that led to the "Judgment of Paris" that led Helen to Troy, which then precipitated the Trojan War which was won by the clever Trojan Horse. Who Knew? And third, if your curiosity has been piqued, then watch *Troy* (with Orlando Bloom as Paris), and if you want to become an Arles/De Milo know-it-all, then read Greg Curtis' *Disarmed*. (How'd I do Aimee, did I keep it brief? ☺)

2. Sacajawea: Sacajawea is the grand dame of Western US exploration. Were it not for her, Lewis and Clark would probably have failed. Sacajawea landed in Portland's Washington Park after being commissioned by

suffragists for the 1905 Lewis and Clark Exposition.

As for a Hot-or-Not angle on *Sacajawea*, the PDX statue is fairly unremarkable, but

there's a new-ish statue of her gracing the Cascade Locks waterfront park beside the Sternwheeler building (in the Gorge, of course). This statue hots it up with a bit of anatomical correctness. Bring a flash camera. Wow, both anatomically and politically correct—that's all "right" by us!

3. Joy: Yikes. *Joy*, or sometimes *Pioneer Woman*, gives personification to the phrase, "good from afar, but far from good." Ole Fred Littman, while not busy teaching sculpture at the Reed/PNCAI/PSU, had a go himself at trying-out a new sculptural material for *Joy*. Sheet bronze was a brand-new medium when he tried to employ it for *Joy*, and in his notes he says, "it

was difficult to work with." Um, yup, it looks like it must've been hard to work with. Did he give up before she was done? Apparently he tired of trying to make her hand look human, so he left it Terminator-like. As for the baby's face, well, as they say, it's a face only a cyborg mom could love.

Oddly, *Portlandia*'s sculptor Ray Kaskey did a very similar mother/child for the city of Charlotte. Whew though, Ray definitely hotted-up his mom. She's so joyous she doesn't even know her top fell off. (Google Image "Sculptures on the Square, Future, Raymond Kaskey" or check our website).

4. Skidmore's Maidens: Two nearly-identical Greek goddesses support Skidmore's Fountain. The 1888 fountain is Portland's oldest public art. You'd think the vision of two maidens adorned in dripping togas would be hot, but alas these gals have dour expressions, possibly because

they were rooting for Henry Weinhard's plan to pipe beer into the fountain for its gala 1888 unveiling. Sadly the beer never flowed—no such riches for you, good citizen. Look sharp, the maidens aren't identical and it's arguable which of the two is hotter.

5. Kvinneakt: *Kvinneakt*, or "nude woman" in Norwegian, is Portland's most-viewed piece of public art <u>EVER</u>, thanks to her starring role in the famed million-selling *Expose Yourself to Art* poster. The short-waisted (Aimee's description ☺) and brazenly nude *Kvinneakt* caused a minor editorial-page fervor at her 1978 unveiling and it's still funny today to watch people react to her gleaming boobs. She's definitely well-loved after all these years, as demonstrated by her shiny nipples and her smoothed-down '70s bush. See also entry C9 for her original *Expose* placement.

6. Caryatids of Pioneer Courthouse: Caryatids are out of fashion nowadays, but Greek buildings were once rife with alluringly clad females propping up building facades, just like the two on Skidmore Fountain. At the courthouse, just inside the door at the 6th street entrance, are two larger-than-life topless "female" wooden caryatids. These "gals," dating to 1884, were moved here from the magnificent iron-clad Kamm Building that was torn down when Harbor Drive was being built in 1948. Whew, we lost the Kamm Building, but at least these "beauties" were saved. Step inside the door for a quick peek and expect the courthouse security guys there to be puzzled at your curiosity.

7. Quest: Three, four, or five groins in this fountain? See entry A4 for the answer.

8. Portlandia: Oh *Portlandia*, our queen. Great granddaughter of iconic trident-wielding Britannia, distant cousin of young bare-breasted Zealandia. Oh *Portlandia* our queen, how fair art thou? With hand clenched upon Neptune's talisman and hair billowing with the Pacific's kiss, our queen suffers no fools, yet extends a hand of friendship down to Portland's plaid-clad masses. But still…to be judged hot or to be judged not, that is the question? In *Portlandia*'s case it isn't adequate to judge her beauty by gazing up at her forever-hard-to-see Portland Building perch. No mon frère, if you dare to stand in judgment of *Portlandia*'s "hot," then you must visit at least

one of the mini-*Portlandias* to get a 360° perspective on her charms—fondle her hidden back foot, take her hand in yours, feel the barbs of her trident, caress the folds of her toga (entry A5). You must judge fairly…

go forth to touch and feel, and if you're the curious type, then even give *Portlandia* a thorough learning before you judge (App 6).

9. Shemanski Fountain: The statue that adorns this fountain is known as *Rebecca at the Well*, from the biblical tale. And well well whaddaya know, this unlikely fountain/statue is the most boob-riffic in PDX, but

not for the reasons you'd imagine. 'Tis true though, Shemanski's got more breast than even *Quest*. The first two breasts belong to diminutive little Rebecca, the biblical waif who graces the fountain's central pedestal. Confoundingly, Rebecca isn't easy to see, even up close, because she hides herself in the fountain's shadows just like she hid her beauty from Isaac before their wedding. But give her a close look and notice her coquettish smile. Apparently some water spilled from her jug as she watered the camels and made her gown quite form-fitting. As if she doesn't know. No wonder Isaac was pleased.

Boob-riffic though? Hardly, you might think, as li'l Becky can barely fill a thimble. But oh ye doubtful ones, cast your glance around the fountain's base and you'll see the smorgas-boobs. Hark, a bevy of big-breasted birds. These are Harpies, a mythic beast endowed with the chest and head of a woman and the wings and feet of an eagle. Never heard of a Harpy? Then get your Google on and search "Harpy Game of Thrones." Personally, we're hoping, in the yet-unwritten books of the series, maybe Daenerys will shape-shift into a lovely bare-breasted harpy and *Alis Volat Propriis* with her own dragons.

10. Mistrals 1, 2, & 3: Frederic Littman, famed Portland sculptor (check online Oregon Encyclopedia), is well-known (well, not very) for his series of four "floating goddesses of the winds." (The fourth is *Farewell to Orpheus*.) Of the other three, only one, *Mistral #2* is on public display—on a high pedestal in the sculpture patio outside the Art Museum. Look for the floating blob of bronze. *Mistral #3* is inside the Keller Auditorium up on the 2nd floor and only visible to people attending an event. This #3 version received some fleeting fame when it was suggested as a possible *"Portlandia"* statue during

the 1982 *Portlandia* design competition (jurors wanted to see some <u>local</u> submissions).

Mistral #1 may be the most interesting to Xccentrics, yet it isn't viewable, as it is owned by the private Vollum Estate. This *Mistral*, named *Mother and Child*, depicts the usual floating goddess, but this time the goddess holds a baby balanced on her airborne thigh—sort of like a *Farewell to Baby* pose.

What's most interesting is that this sculpture was stolen from the estate in 2008 and cut up into bits for meth-head scrap value...but then amazingly recovered by the police. The Vollum Estate took the recovered bits and had them re-welded and re-mounted in their garden, but alas, she was but a shadow of her former self...it was farewell to her legs and farewell to her baby too. In a surprising PDXtra odd twist to this story, the local band Menomena was recording an album at the Vollum Estate in 2010 when they saw the peculiar re-welded franken-statue. They took its photo, and surprise, made it the cover of their "Mines" album. Whoa! (*Oregonian* articles and photos of the mistrals and the theft/recovery on our website).

11. Farewell to Orpheus: *Farewell to Orpheus* is Portland's nudest statue. Full feminine form on full frontal display. For all her floating 'n' flaunting though, she isn't well-known outside of South Park blocks locals. Is this possibly due to the statue's funny name...or perhaps her funny shape? Instead of sculptor Littman calling her by her name, Eurydice, Littman clevered-up and named her after the Greek myth staring Orpheus and his girlfriend. The mythic tales differ as to exactly what happened back in the day, but basically Eurydice was snake-bit and died and boyfriend Orpheus was so sad over her death that he pleaded with the gods for her return from

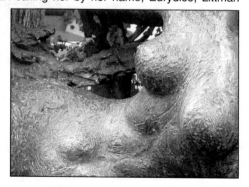

the underworld. Hades said "OK," but put a tricky condition upon her release. Up they went, happily on their way out of the Underworld until Orpheus screwed up the plan and Eurydice was swept back downwards, casting a sorrowful *"Farewell to Orpheus"* look as she drifted back into eternal darkness.

So maybe the tricksy name is to blame for her lack of fans. Or maybe it has to do with the odd belly Littman crafted for her. He didn't use models, but rather sculpted his females "from memory." Hmmm, it kind of looks like Eurydice spent her time in Hades doing mad sit-ups and crunches, perhaps knowing that Orpheus liked a tight 6-pack. But who was the woman Littman conjured "from memory" with those unnatural ab-bumps?

12. The Dreamer: *The Dreamer* is a reclining nude woman upon a pedestal in the middle of Pettygrove Park's reflective pool. This woman is all curves, glowing golden tan, and a heart of gold. Manuel Izquierdo, longtime professor emeritus at PNW College of Art, said his sculpture *The Dreamer*, "speaks of hope, beauty and serenity...of love, and for a better life in our midst." Hmmm, that's a mouthful, but then he's an artist, right? A more fanciful description is given by Roger Hull (professor, art historian and Izquierdo author) on the Izquierdo Oregon Encyclopedia website. "*The Dreamer*...organic and voluptuous, it is a modern river goddess. Izquierdo's faultlessly prop-welded seams...give the piece a taut clarity despite its sensuousness." Huh...can we get a translation of that art-speak please?

Well, in spite of—or possibly in celebration of—*The Dreamer's* taut clarity...if you splash through the pool you can hop up and "hope for a better life" by having a seat on her face... if, hahaha, you can figure out which end of her is her face.

13. Vera Katz: Vera Katz didn't become mayor of Portland from 1993 to 2005 by looking model-esque. She was a popular mayor because she got important stuff done. Thus, don't expect some artsy "feminine grace" statue to honor Vera...nope, expect an exact likeness of a true achiever. Look around...are there any other PDex-mayor statues around Portland? Nope. Vera is the only one. During her three-term tenure she crafted into existence the very Eastbank

Esplanade her likeness now sits on. If you walk the Esplanade, sit and give Vera a hug because if it weren't for her, we wouldn't even have this Esplanade to walk on. For PDXtra Vera Katz intrigue, see "Maillol Nudes" hot-or-not.

14. The Dream: You might not think that a female figure on a statue representing Dr. Martin Luther King "stepping forward to deliver his message to the world" would be a likely candidate for "hot." Well, think again, because it seems that before the woman joined Martin upon this pedestal it looks as if she went swimming in her dress and now strides forth into a stiff breeze. Yeah, Martin, I bet you have a dream!

15. Ideals: This hollow-faced, full-figured gal strides forth towards...???... unknown ideals. Artist Muriel Castanis has crafted many similar sculptures for installations the world over, yet despite their popularity people seem to have a love/hate relationship with them. We Xccentrics aren't sure which ideals Castanis is trying to express with this not-so-friendly ghost, but our friend Dave, upon first sighting of *Ideals*, exclaimed in his best Borat voice, "sleeve of wizard!"

16. Holladay Gardener: This statue commemorates a beloved "neighborhood gardener" and community activist. Chances are that this is the <u>only</u> female statue you'll ever see depicted wearing a sweatshirt and holding a pair of blackberry clippers in her hand. Very Portland.

17. Joan of Arc: Oh heaven-sent Joan, hail the 19-year-old virgin who lead the French army to remarkable victories over the occupying British legions. Her secret was…a-ha…she was a minion of God. That always helps. Our Joan, gifted to the city in 1924, has the easier task of simply guarding the large Coe traffic circle at NE Cesar Chavez and Glisan, named after Joan's benefactor. For years Joan was camouflaged in patina-green, but in 2009 RACC ushered in the gilded age, making our Joan as shiny as many of her statuesque sisters around the globe. Our Joan isn't unique, having at least five twin sisters scattered around the world, the most famed being at Paris' Place des Pyramides. If you're keen to see a bit of her old green, then check the art-museum alcove in the Portland Building. To our knowledge, the only mention of our Joan, in either film or song, is in Sleater-Kinney's *Light Rail Coyote* (D11).

APPENDIX 2
Custom Bike Racks

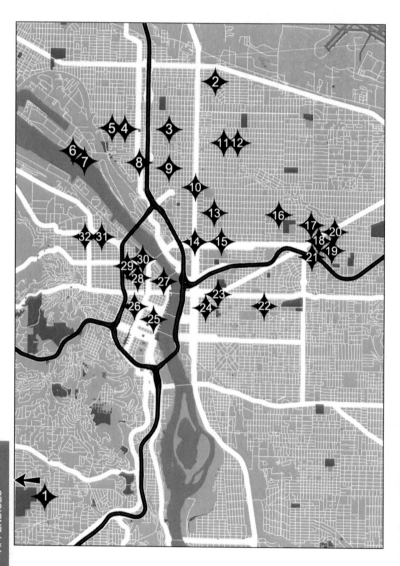

182

1. **Cruiser Meltdown:** Pertrich's, 23915 SW Scholls Ferry Road
2. **Big Bike:** Village Ballroom, 700 NE Dekum
3. **Sunflowers:** N Commercial and Killingsworth
4. **Coffee Cups:** Atomic Pizza, 1936 N Killingsworth St
5. **Dog and Cat:** Overlook Veterinary Hospital, 1936 N Killingsworth St
6. **Truckin':** Daimler, 4747 N Channel Ave at entrance
7. **Wheel:** Daimler, 4747 N Channel Ave parking lot side
8. **Easter Island:** Alibi, 4024 N Interstate Ave
9. **Nerd Glasses:** Myoptic, 3978 N Williams Ave
10. **She and Him:** Planned Parenthood, 3727 NE MLK Jr Blvd.
11. **Penny Farthing:** Frock, 1439 NE Alberta
12. **Fruit and Veggie:** Alberta Co-op, 1500 NE Alberta
13. **WWJD:** Lutheran Church, 2710 NE 14th
14. **Coffee Cups:** Tiny's, 2031 NE MLK Jr Blvd.
15. **Fork and Spoon:** Milo's City Café, 1325 NE Broadway
16. **Braces:** Dr. Safirstein, 2707 NE 33rd Ave
17. **Toothbrush and Floss:** Eilers Dental, 2115 NE 42nd Ave
18. **Hollywood Stars:** Hollywood Plaza, NE 42nd and Sandy
19. **Stethoscope:** Broadway Medical Clinic, 4212 NE Broadway
20. **Hollywood:** Hollywood Theater, 4122 NE Sandy Blvd.
21. **Glamor Glasses:** Hollywood District, NE 40th and Sandy
22. **www:** Value CAD Mapping, 26th and NE Ankeny
23. **Mt. Climber:** Portland Rock Gym, 21 NE 12th
24. **Headphones:** KBOO, 20 SE 8th Ave.
25. **Scales of Justice:** Swanson, Thomas, Coon & Newton, 820 SW 2nd
26. **Eggbeater:** Saint Cupcake, 1138 SW Morrison
27. **Lily Pad:** Lan Su Chinese Garden, 239 NW Everett St.
28. **Nice Grill:** Parking Lot, NW 12th and Hoyt
29. **Leaf Covered Parking:** PNCA, 1241 NW Johnson
30. **Fremont Bridges:** (see entry B2)
31. **Gears:** 2552 NW Vaughn
32. **Industrial bits:** Industrial Saloon, 2572 NW Vaughn

We described the origins of Portland's custom bike racks in entry B2. For the past twenty years these artistic bike rack creations have been slowly appearing all over Portland, and now even around the nation. We Xccentrics applaud every business who has spent their own money to creatively enhance our public sidewalks while also giving a new PDX meaning to the comment "nice rack."

The map for this appendix shows the custom one-of-a-kind racks that we are aware of as of 2014. Surely there are many more out there, but no records are kept by PBOT, so we have no idea just how many or where they are. If you know of one that we've missed, please send us an email with an address and photo so we can try to collect them all and give a pat on the back to every deserving business. On our website we'll have a link to an online GoogleMap which we'll keep as current as we're able. Also, three cheers for Merrill Denney!

APPENDICES

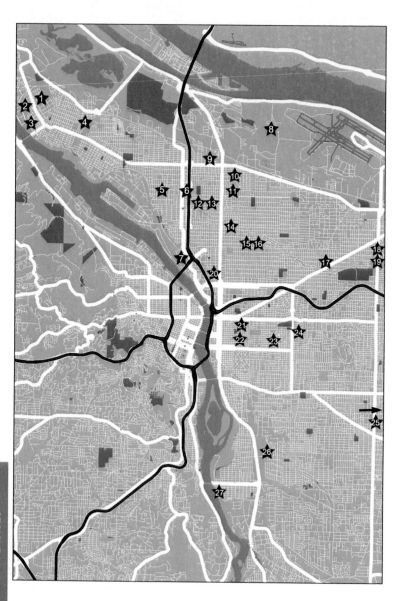

1. N St Johns & Central
2. N St Johns & Syracuse
3. N Edison & St. Louis
4. N Gilbert & Sedro
5. N Wilbur & Holman
6. N Holman & Maryland
7. N Concord & Overlook
8. NE Sunderland Drive at Dignity Village
9. N Williams & Russet
10. NE 8th & Holland
11. NE 8th & Holman
12. N Killingsworth Court & Borthwick
13. N Haight & Emerson
14. NE 6th & Going
15. NE 11th & Beech
16. NE 13th & Beech
17. NE 57th & Stanton
18. NE 86th and Beech
19. NE 86th and Milton
20. N Tillamook & Rodney
21. SE 16th & Ash
22. SE 15th & Alder
23. SE 33rd & Yamhill (Sunnyside Piazza)
24. SE 42nd & Morrison
25. SE 130th Pl & Ramona
26. SE 37th & Bybee
27. SE 9th & Sherret (Share-it-Square Sellwood)

APPENDICES

continued ➡

Neighborhood community-building intersection art began in 1996 at Sellwood's Sherett and 9th intersection. The neighbors there, fed up with a rampant crime wave of speeding and jaywalking, banded-together to take back their streets, while maybe getting to know one another a bit better too. The neighbors met, talked, laughed, schemed, and finally decided to paint their intersection with flowers and trees and butterflies, build funky benches, and give away free tea. "Share-It Square" was born!

Share-It Square from Google Earth 2009

Wait a minute though. City officials were not pleased by this rogue band arting-up the public space and street—this was against policy. Hilariously, a city official told the Share-It rebels, in all seriousness, "This is a public space—nobody can use it." Hahaha, the irony (this is now our favorite-ever PDX quote). In another city the rebel uprising might have been quashed by the Powers. But this is Portland and Share-It Square had the formidable do-gooder Mark Lakeman on its side. The Powers backed-down, the policy got changed, and good spread over the land.

Share-It Square free tea and relaxation station

NE 8th & Holman

Nowadays, intersection murals are all over Portland. Lakeman, heady with his victory over the wonks, formed a non-profit called City Repair to facilitate neighborhood art-activism. City Repair has put on gala annual Halloween parties called "Howl" to raise funds. The word spread throughout the city and now there are new intersection murals popping up every summer, just like new tattoos on the arms of our baristas.

Us PDXccentrics like to tour the intersection arts in two different ways. First, we bike/drive around and look with our eyes and cameras. We call this "eye-looking" and it's fun because, like a treasure hunt, you get to go places and see stuff that regular day-to-day driving rarely highlights. The

NE 12th & Beech

second way to see intersection murals is via Google Earth. Just plunk the street names into the search box and you'll "fly there" for a sweet Goog's-eye view. We call this "Google-looking." Add the Street View icon onto the scene and oh what stay-at-home fun you'll have. Google and intersection art are like a Reese's Peanut Butter Cup—two great things that go great together. Yum.

SE 42nd & Morrison

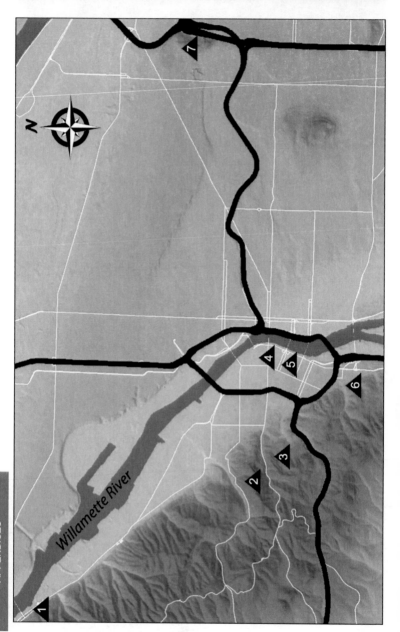

1. **St. Johns Bridge from Ridge Trail:** NW Bridge Ave. Parking just south of the St. Johns Bridge (entry D4).

2. **Pittock Mansion:** 3229 NW Pittock Drive.

3. **Washington Park:** 611 SW Kingston Ave.

4. **Portland City Grill:** 111 SW 5th Ave. 30th floor of the US Bancorp Tower (Big Pink).

5. **Departure Restaurant:** 525 SW Morrison St., in The Nines Hotel.

6. **Aerial Tram:** 3303 SW Bond St.

7. **Rocky Butte:** NE Rocky Butte Rd.

APPENDICES

St. Johns Bridge/Cathedral Park. See Entry D3 for directions to the viewpoint trail. By far the city's most beautiful bridge with the most beautiful bridge views too. Free.

Pittock Mansion. 3229 NW Pittock Dr. The classic mansion became a city park after nearly being lost to the 1962 Columbus Day Storm. Great views of downtown and Mt. Hood from the mansion's 900-foot hilltop. The Pittock is a Hollywood fave, appearing in *First Love*, *Unhinged,* and *Body of Evidence* (See Flicks list), and also *The Favor*, *Little Blue Pill*, and *Ghost of Sarah Hardy*. View is free, admission inside about $10 per person.

Washington Park Rose Test Garden. 400 SW Kingston Ave. Historic WWI roots. Epic view over downtown while you stop to smell the roses. Free.

Portland Aerial Tram. 3303 SW Bond Ave. Just a few bucks each to take an exciting 4-minute ride up and then back down. Linger at the top as long as you want. Best views are from the east end of the tram car...mountains, river, bridges, city...and more!

Portland City Grill. 111 SW 5th Ave. Located on the 30th floor of the US Bancorp Tower (Big Pink), the City Grill is Portland's highest restaurant. The spacious interior sports ooh-la-la 270° views of the not-sprawling city below and mountains, rivers, and forest to the horizons. The happy hour is legend…watching the city lights pop on whilst the pianist tinkles the ivories with both faves and quirky covers. Expect a crowd, as this place is deservedly popular.

Departure Restaurant. 525 SW Morrison. Perched on the 15th floor atop The Nines Hotel building, Departure offers a view straight down onto Pioneer Courthouse Square, as well as far and wide to the east and south. Unlike Portland City Grill, Departure has outdoor tables on airy patios. Not as crowded as its Big Pink neighbor….which is nice, but 'tis a bit spendier.

Rocky Butte. 3341 NE Rocky Butte Rd. The 360° view from 614-foot butte isn't that eye-boggling, but being atop Rocky Butte is just plain neat. Rocky Butte is sort of like an outdoor castle, the rock ramparts constructed by the WPA in the 1930s. Sweet sunset watching! Free.

APPENDIX 5
Portland's Beerginnings

A lot has been written about Portland being the epicenter for America's craft-brew revolution. Most brewpubs in the world...yada-yada. There's also a "tun" of online sources that'll give you a good brief sketch of the early-'80s beginnings of Portland's beervana, or, if you are a keen beer geek who's interested in the details of the beervana story, then you'll definitely want to read Pete Dunlop's 2013 *Portland Beer* which tells the whole story in spirited and accurate fashion.

Here at PDXccentral we don't want to regurgitate the familiar story. We want to go a bit deeper than the "usual story" and give you some local-secret tips so that you can self-tour the two compact areas of PDX that represent the ground-zero spots which sprouted the world-famous craft-brew wonderland the *Willamette Week* first called "Beervana" back in 1994. But first...we feel we need to give a solid shout-out to a couple of oft-forgotten craft-brewing pioneers as well as giving due credit to the four Portland upstarts who kicked the craft-brew revolution into high gear in the mid 1980s: BridgePort, Widmer, McMenamins, and Portland Brewing.

The first little-known pioneer of Oregon's craft-brewing history is Charles "Chuck" Coury. Chuck was an early-day Willamette Valley vintner, and also an avid homebrewer. In 1979, after leaving the wine biz, Chuck and his wife Shirley made the leap to create Oregon's first micro-brewery, naming it after Shirley's maiden name. **Cartwright Brewing** became the first brewery to open in Oregon since Prohibition (and the second in the nation). Cartwright should be celebrated as legend, but instead is forgotten by most everyone except old beer nuts.

Oregon Journal 3-12-1979

True enough, Chuck wasn't successful in his attempt to brew/bottle/sell *Cartwright Beer*, but he definitely got the ball rolling for those who would learn from his mistakes and follow in his footsteps. Pete Dunlop in *Portland Beer* remarks, "After Henry Weinhard, Charles Coury may have been the most important brewer in Oregon History" (p.77). On OPB's excellent must-see *Beervana* video, no less than Mike McMenamin and

Dick Ponzi (BridgePort) lavish praise on Chuck, calling him a "visionary." (At minute 16 the *Beervana* video also shows super-rare film of the Cartwright Brewery in action!) Cartwright closed on New Year's 1982 after 18 months of financially-plagued existence (poor beer quality too). Local homebrewers, who had cheered his pioneer effort, were disappointed, but the necessary seed was sown. Deliverance was at hand for Oregon's craft brewing revolution.

The second nearly-forgotten pioneer was Yakima's **Bert Grant**. Grant was a lifelong beer industry insider and hops specialist. When Washington State ironed-out its brewpub laws in mid-1982 (3 years before Oregon) Bert quickly opened America's first brewpub, beating Redhook by mere weeks. Yakima Brewing and Malting (oft-known as Grant's) was born July 1982. Grant differed from many 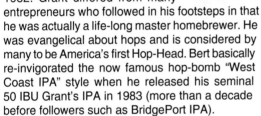 entrepreneurs who followed in his footsteps in that he was actually a life-long master homebrewer. He was evangelical about hops and is considered by many to be America's first Hop-Head. Bert basically re-invigorated the now famous hop-bomb "West Coast IPA" style when he released his seminal 50 IBU Grant's IPA in 1983 (more than a decade before followers such as BridgePort IPA).

Anyone interested in the eccentric origins of craft-brewing should read Bert's beer-biography *The Ale Master*—a brief and engaging profile of a true craftsman pioneer hop-wizard. Sadly, Bert died in 2001 and his Yakima brewpub withered and died in 2004 without his charismatic presence. Cheers to Bert, a legend we tip our hops to!

Four Brewers of the Ale-pocalypse
BridgePort: Widmer: McMenamins: Portland Brewing

After Cartwright folded on 1/1/82 it basically took 2 more years to get things brewing again in Portland. Meanwhile, the success of Grant's and Redhook Ales in 1982/83 proved that the people of the northwest had a taste for flavorful craft-ales. The years 1984/85 were when the Portland craft-brew revolution really took seed, thanks to the four landmark brew teams who took the leap: BridgePort, Widmer, McMenamins, and Portland Brewing.

Not only did these brewsmen begin breweries, they also banded-together to successfully petition the Oregon Legislature to amend the Prohibition-era law that forbade breweries from operating pubs (law amended 7/85). This legendary story of comraderie amongst the soon-to-be-rivals is best documented in OPB's *Beervana*, or more-detailed in Dunlop's *Portland Beer*.

BridgePort Brewing. Pioneer Willamette Valley vintners Dick and Nancy Ponzi hired Karl Ockert and together established Columbia River Brewing (now BridgePort) in a run-down area of NW Portland. The brewery opened in 11/84 and the onsite brewpub two years later in 1986. Thus BridgePort is now the oldest operating craft brewery in Oregon, in addition to being housed in its original start-up location—the 1887 Portland Cordage rope-factory building at NW 13th and Marshall.

Nowadays there isn't much to see that harkens back to BridgePort's birth…except one very large visual icon. The giant clock above the bar (in the original pub room) has its hands forever stopped at 4 and 11, with a date painted below in Roman numerals. Sure enough, this is the date the Ponzi's established Columbia River Brewing and began fabricating the brewery 4/11/1984.

Widmer Brewing. Kurt and Rob Widmer, along with their father Ray, took inspiration from Cartwright Brewing and began piecemeal assembly of their brewery on a shoestring budget in 1984, just a block from BridgePort in what is now a Key Bank building at 14th and Lovejoy. The Widmers consider their brewery "founded" in April 1984, though they didn't begin selling their first "Alt Bier" until April 1985. Today there is nothing Widmer-esque to

see at the original Widmer ground-zero location, but it is fun to match-up old Widmer photos with the bank building of today (pix on their website or ours). The brothers Wid moved their brewery to N. Russell St. in 1990 also changing their name from Widmer Brewing to Widmer Brothers. They opened their first brewpub, the Gasthaus, in 1995. On the walls/bathroom/gift shop at the Gasthaus you can see some photos of the original brewery and you might be able to have a pint of their first brew "Alt Bier" from the tap.

McMenamins. Brothers Mike and Brian were already multi-pub owners when the PDX brewvolution began, actually helping along the revolution by serving Cartwright's bottled beers as well as early draft ales from Bert Grant and Redhook. The McMenamins uber-successful brewpub empire, now famously entrenched in the eccentric landscape of Portland, has two locations especially notable in reference to Portland's beerginnings.

Barley Mill Pub. This is the oldest McMenamins pub, dating to 6/1983. Especially interesting about this ground-zero location is that it was named for the antique barley mill that the brothers bought from the closed-down Cartwright Brewery. Whoa, this machine had its teeth on the first-ever micro-brewed barley in Oregon, and, as far as we know, it's the only remnant of Cartwright to be seen. This still-operational contraption stands in honor in the center of the pub and is still used yearly to mill malted barley for special brews—sort of a "grind-zero" at McMenamins ground-zero! And… since this oldest pub takes its name from a historic artifact you might say this is also ground-zero for the whole concept of the McMenamins preserving/honoring local history in their brewpubs.

Hillsdale Brewery and Public House. This unpretentious pub in SW Portland is actually the <u>first</u> brewpub opened in all of Oregon. After the McMenamins helped get the brewpub law changed in 7/85, the brothers hired a brewer and began brewing/serving at this location first, at least partially to do with a floor drain which was already in place from the previous Skipper's fish and chips shop. The hand-written recipe for Oregon's first batch of legal brewpub beer is framed near the side door and on the walls and coasters you can see a depiction of Hillsdale's original copper brew kettle.

Portland Brewing. After consulting with Bert Grant, Portland Brewing opened its brewpub in Jan 1986. They began by producing Grant's beers on contract before launching their own Portland Ale and subsequently moving on to a greater fame with MacTarnahan's Ale. The brewpub at 14th and Flanders in now home to Rogue Pub/Distillery but there are still some relics of the Portland Brewing pub to be seen. First, below the front door you'll see the original name

and date tiled into the entranceway. Then inside the bar room is a large framed photo of the original Portland Brewing Pub taken from the very corner where the photo now hangs. Neat—look for the piano overhang, skylight and light fixture from way back when.

Beervana Timeline Snapshot

1965:	Fritz Maytag buys Anchor Brewing, San Francisco CA
1976-82:	New Albion Brewery, Sonoma CA
1980-82:	Cartwright Brewing, Portland OR
1981-now:	Sierra Nevada Brewing, Chico CA
7/1982:	Yakima Brewing (Grant's), nation's first brewpub, Yakima WA
8/1982:	Redhook Brewery, Seattle WA
11/1984:	Columbia River Brewing (BridgePort) opens, Portland OR
4/1985:	Widmer Brewing opens, Portland OR
7/1985:	Oregon brewpub bill signed into law.
11/1985:	McMenamins Hillsdale becomes first OR brewpub
1/1986:	Portland Brewing brewpub opens, Portland OR
3/1986:	BridgePort pub opens.
1988:	First Oregon Brewers Festival
1994:	*Willamette Week* coins "Beervana"

APPENDIX 6
How Portlandia

The concept of *"Portlandia"* began with the 1980 design of the Portland Building, but the inspiration for the female figure of *Portlandia* dates from a century earlier on the 1878 City Seal of Portland. The City Seal obviously came first, but like the chicken and the egg, without the Portland Building we wouldn't have either a statue or the name *Portlandia*. So let's begin the saga of *Portlandia* with the Portland Building.

The name *"Portlandia"* originates with architect Michael Graves—the first person known to coin the name. In 1980 Graves had entered a city-sponsored competition to design/build a new Portland Public Services Building (later shortened to Portland Building). National-caliber architects were solicited for design proposals. The contest was whittled down to Graves and two other finalists. The other finalists proposed smaller "modern" buildings akin to boxy glass structures with fountains adorning the front plaza. Graves went "post-modern," his design harkening back to Classic times when buildings had ornamentation and character built into the structure rather than just having some art out front in the plaza. In addition to Graves' colorful design, he also designed the entrance portico to be topped by a monumental figurative sculpture of the classical tradition rather than the quizzical modern sculpture of the day. Graves named this yet-to-be-designed sculpture *"Portlandia,"* and he saw her as the embodiment of "Lady Commerce" from the Portland City Seal (see entry A5-6). Graves' "temple-like" design won the competition, helped mightily by the fact that his design was both bigger and less expensive than his competitors. Portland wanted more building-for-the-buck as well as a unique design that would surely make America stand up and take notice of Portland.

Upon winning the building commission, Graves and the city council formed a citizen Art Selection Committee which would then use the new "1% for the Arts" funds available ($220,000) to solicit sculpture designs via another nationwide competition. They compiled an art-submission prospectus that showed the building, the City Seal and a mock-up of how Graves envisioned the statue. Artists were instructed to send in drawings of potential art pieces as well as a descriptive paragraph about their concept.

The response was large, over 200 entries! The Committee was specifically looking for figurative/allegorical sculptures with themes from the City Seal. The entries were soon whittled down to five. The five chosen semi-finalists were then given a couple thousand dollars each to produce miniature mock-up of their proposals (around 2-3 feet tall). They were also asked for a detailed description of their theme, an outline of the materials and a proposed budget for the final work of art.

Here are the five models delivered to the Art Selection Committee in April 1982, with comments by the artists.

Cascieri Sculpture Group, New York

"Portlandia sits on a land-scape of waves and clouds, symbolic of her location near ocean and mountains. She has a backdrop of the cogwheel representing her roots in the commerce of the city."

Oregon Journal 4/22/1982

Cascieri Group

Frudakis and Hesness, Philadelphia

"In one hand Portlandia bears the trident representing the predominant importance of a maritime economy to the existence of the city. The other hand extends a rose, symbol of the Rose City, with its museums, universities and cultural institutions. By holding both items, Portlandia indicates the importance of establishing a harmony between cultural and economic values in society. The figure stands on the bow of a ship which moves through waves of water, wheat and fir branches, symbolizing the continuing importance of agriculture, forest and maritime aspects of Portland's growth."

Frudakis

Oregon Journal 4/22/1982

Penelope Jenks, Boston

"The figure of Portlandia will be emerging from the building… with attached to the hands—one to a trident continuing out of the building, the other holding a sheaf of wheat."

Jenks

Oregon Journal 4/22/1982

Richard Savini, Washington D.C.

"The sculpture's motifs are formed as an expression of the building's architectural narratives, and further, the motifs make direct references to the characteristics of the Portland environment: the mountains on its horizons; its waterways and procession of its beautiful Columbia River Gorge; its hilltop views, and the spectacular clouds of its skies that seem to make of it a city 'in' the sky. The pose of the figure with its elated draperies and the garden gate motif are used in the classical sense as they refer to transcendence and the unity of contrasts."

Savini

Oregon Journal 4/22/1982

Raymond Kaskey, Washington D.C.

"I decided to stick with the idea of a wind-blown figure. It suggested sea breezes and seemed a good symbol of the city of Portland."

From the five semi-finalist mock-up submissions the budgetary and weight constraints of using metal on so big of a sculpture became apparent. All five mainly used reinforced fiberglass with some metal flourishes. It became clear that wanting monumentally big, yet light-weight, was not easy on a $200,000 budget. Some entries offered the use of copper or bronze, but at a significantly higher budget.

Kaskey

Oregon Journal 4/22/1982

Thus, after a review period, the committee chose two finalists—Kaskey and Savini. But, they were far from happy with their two finalists. Both sculptures proposed reinforced and painted fiberglass. The committee wanted "further refinements" to each entry and sent the two finalists "back to the drawing board" with a slew of comments. Both Kaskey and Savini were given about three months to refine their offering in terms of modifications, materials and budget…and then to re-submit a finalized model for the ultimate selection.

Inspirations for *Portlandia*

Raymond Kaskey: Kaskey stated that his inspiration for *Portlandia*'s crouched pose was the painting "*Ancient of Days*" by William Blake. In this painting "God" crouches down from the heavens on one knee, hair billowing sideways in the wind and reaching downwards with a compass-like device. Kaskey commented that he liked this "tight bit of geometry" because it would allow him to get more statue into the allotted space—a crouched 50-foot woman rather than a slender 30-foot woman.

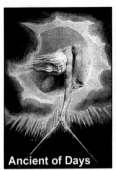
Ancient of Days

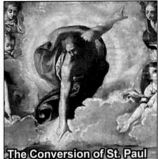
The Conversion of St. Paul

A second inspiration came from an art-book photo that Kaskey has since donated to the National Building Museum with his *Portlandia* archives. This art book page not only shows *Ancient of Days*, but also a cropped version of Teddeo Zucarri's "*The Conversion of St. Paul.*" Here we have God zapping Paul off his horse while also reaching back and upwards with his other hand. Wow, one look at these paintings side-by-side and Kaskey's inspiration becomes clear.

Richard Savini: Savini's inspiration is less clear, but the *Oregon Journal* commented that it evoked the goddess Nike in her famous "*Winged Victory*" pose, gown blown against her torso as she strides forward. Whoa, imagine the Goddess Nike as Portland's civic personification—ha, that sure would've melded our commercial interests with our allegorical!

Nike

In August 1982 the final models were put on display in the lobby of the Portland Building...and the favorite quickly became apparent. Savini extensively re-worked his *Portlandia* figurine as well as the V-shaped backdrop relief, but to no avail. If anything, the committee disliked it more than the previous model, commenting simply "too busy." Kaskey, on the other hand, made great strides forward with his new version. First he removed the wreath from *Portlandia*'s down-reaching hand and replaced it with a beckoning and friendly gesture—a big hit with the committee! Even more impressive was that Kaskey now offered to construct the entire 38-foot monument out of hammered copper, a-la the Statue of Liberty. Whoa, that impressed the committee, especially since Savini only offered to use bronze at an $80k increase in expense. Thus, Kaskey's final entry took a huge step forward while Savini's revised entry stepped backwards. The decision was made—the Portland Building would have a hammered-copper goddess from the hand of Raymond Kaskey.

For the rest of the tale...from fabrication to delivery to nationwide publicity...we have an extensive saga of Portlandia on our website. The story is interesting, at least to us PDXccentrics, but it ended up being much more than we wanted to squeeze into this li'l guidebook.

INDEX

INDEX

Check out our other great guidebooks!

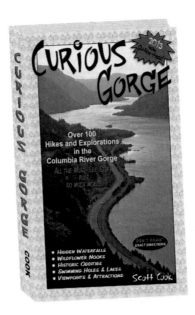

Amazon reviews are always appreciated!